T0146850

Ignatius Ekpenyong Idio, Sr.

A Memoir: The Intriguing Journey of My Life

Dr. Ignatius E. Idio, Sr.

authorHOUSE®

AuthorHouse™
1663 Liberty Drive
Bloomington, IN 47403
www.authorhouse.com
Phone: 833-262-8899

Published by AuthorHouse 11/24/2023

ISBN: 978-1-5049-4752-7 (sc)
ISBN: 978-1-5049-4751-0 (e)

Library of Congress Control Number: 2015914301

Print information available on the last page.

This book is printed on acid-free paper.

DEDICATION

To the people who nurtured me -

MY GRANDMOTHER, ADIAHA NKENTA
Who was the pillar throughout my life;
MY MOTHER, AKON
Who paid the ultimate sacrifice for me;
MY FATHER, FRANCIS
Whose kindness to others made me the beneficiary;
MY CHILDREN
IGNATIUS, JR., FRANCISCA, STEPHANIE,
VICTORIA & THEIR CHILDREN
Who will sustain the family name *[Idio]* as an
eternal legacy from one generation to the next;
and
MY K-GRADUATE SCHOOL TEACHERS
Whose counseling and mentorship sustained my desire to succeed.

If I had my way –

Teachers would be the highest paid professionals in every country of the world because they have the power to change life one student at a time. Teachers teach the presidents, the corporate executives, the medical doctors and scientists, and they teach teachers too.

- Ignatius E. Idio ca. 1 April 2015

CONTENTS

PREQUEL

Every beginning has an end and the end may not have the same setting as the beginning. Everything about my life began at Mbiaya Uruan, a small village in Northern Uruan clan, in Akwa Ibom State of Nigeria, West Africa *(see an overview of Mbiaya Uruan, Akwa Ibom State, Nigeria in Appendix A)*. My life has been full of intriguing events that connived to shape me to be the person I am today. Therefore, I owe my very being to the people who became my surrogate parents and mentors after I was orphaned at a young age.

Back then, Mbiaya Uruan was a vibrant village with a magistrate court, a health center, and a primary school. Most men and women were subsistence farmers, crafts people, and traders. There were also fishermen who made a livelihood by fishing from the tributaries of the Atlantic Ocean, including the riverine areas of Efiat and Oron. Most of the fishermen left their families and camped at their fishing stations for weeks and months. While at the stations, they often sent home fish, crawfish, shrimps, and lobsters to their wives and children. The fishermen also sold their fish to make money. With the money, they bought canoes, fishing nets, and other tools needed for their trades. The Mbiaya people were very hardworking and industrious.

My life success depended on the firm shoulders of my heroes - both alive and dead - upon which I stood as they reached back to give me a hand up. Heroes like Mrs. Unah, my first grade teacher; Uncle Eyo Essien; Barrister Ambassador (Amba) Willis Obong; Dr. Amos Ames (my doctoral study advisor); and Dr. Calixtus Idio (my senior brother). The people who made positive impacts on my life were those who successfully made it to the top of the ladder. Then, they reached down and extended their hands to pull me gently up each rung of the ladder to the top. They all believed that what made them great was reaching back and helping somebody else - like me - to become great. Dr. Calixtus Idio had to put his personal dreams and aspirations temporarily on hold, in order to help release my dreams. This story is an exposé of the intriguing journey of my life. I hope you will enjoy it as you travel along with me. Feel free to be critical but not judgmental.

CHAPTER 1

The Glooms and Glows of My Childhood

Everybody has a story to tell. This is my story. I am one of the 19 children in our family. The exact date of my birth was not documented in the official birth registry or record. In my adolescent years, I made several attempts to obtain my actual date of birth from my relatives who stood in the place of my late parents, but none of them knew exactly the year I was born. It was in 2000 when I visited Nigeria for my traditional marriage to Edemekong Joseph Esema Idio that I happened upon an old photo of my late cousin, who was born in 1952. My elder brother, Calixtus Ime Ekpenyong Idio, speculated that I shared the same birth year with my cousin. Since my official birth certificate was not available at the time I registered at Peace Lutheran Primary School at Abak Ibiaku Uruan, I decided to use October 5, 1954, as my date of birth, and I have since used the same date for all of my other official documents.

My father, Francis Ekpenyong Udokang Akpandem Akana Uyoko, was a polygamist. He had 19 children with 4 wives, including the three of us with my mother, who was the youngest and the last of his wives. Back then, polygamy was culturally acceptable phenomenon among my people. To some extent, polygamy is still a common practice among my people. However, it is often tempered by a man's financial ability to marry more than one wife and the ability to sustain a large family. Back then, a man's wealth was measured by the number of wives he married and the number of children he had. The children supplied the necessary labor to work the farm and raised crops for the family. Married men procreated several children knowing that some of the children will die young from diseases because there were limited and inadequate health care facilities. When my father met my mother, Akon Udoenang Okpok Ekpenyong Idio, she was a young, 5-foot-7-inch, attractive woman. She was attending to her sick aunt (my grandmother's younger sister) who was in the care of my father, a renowned spiritual healer. My father would not have passed up the opportunity to win the heart of this beautiful, elegant 17-year-old. Therefore, my father and my mother fell in love and got married. Following the recovery of his second daughter from her ailment, my maternal grandfather gladly and generously sanctioned the marriage between my father and mother, partly because my father healed his younger daughter and also because my father was popularly known for his spiritual power to heal very sick men and women who were thought to have been possessed by demons and evil spirits. My mother's beauty and grace elicited unrestrained lust, attention, and desire from my father and induced spiteful jealousy in my father's senior wives. The senior wives perceived my mother to be more favored by my father and accused her of getting all the attention, love, and preference. The three senior wives correctly concluded that my father spent more intimate times with my mother than he did with them.

As a young new wife, my mother did not have her own apartment in the family compound. She had to live with the most senior wife until she gave birth to my elder brother, Calixtus Ime Ekpenyong Idio (a medical doctor) on June 21, 1945. Next, my mother gave birth to my sister, Ekpeawan, in 1949, who died later that year. My mother later gave birth to me and then my sister, Lawrencia Ekpenyong Idio-Itiat (a certified teacher). After Calixtus was born, my father decided to build another apartment unit within the big compound for my mother and her children.

As I have alluded to above, my father, Chief Francis Ekpenyong Udokang Akpandem Akana Uyoko *[aka]* Francis Ekpenyong Idio, was a prominent occultist or spiritualist who practiced these arts to heal people who were possessed by spirits or afflicted with different ailments. He had in his possession a very ancient and powerful book titled, *The Sixth and Seventh Books of Moses.* This is "an 18th- or 19th-century magical text allegedly written by <u>Moses</u>, and passed down as hidden (or lost) books of the *Five Books of Moses* or Pentateuch or a <u>grimoire</u> - a text of magical incantations and seals; it purports to instruct the reader in the spells used to create the miracles portrayed in the <u>Judaea-Christian Bible</u>" (Wikipedia). It was not unusual for my father to employ the magical incantations in *The Sixth and Seventh Books of Moses. He* used them to his advantage and for the benefits of his patients who often walked away healed and free of their afflictions.

My father was once a devout practicing Catholic. In fact, he and his first wife were wedded in the Catholic Church. He served as a catechism teacher at Mbiaya Uruan and Eman Uruan Catholic dioceses. But something happened in the church that pitted him against Bishop James Moynagh, S.P.S. (Prefecture Apostolic of Calabar, 1947), which, in my opinion, must have been the reason that compelled the bishop to excommunicate my father from the church. Since the actual event that caused a drift between my father and the church was not written down or recorded for posterity, I can only speculate that his involvement in occultism and possession of *The Sixth and Seventh Books of Moses*, from which he derived most of his healing powers and which was a blatant deviation from the teaching and doctrines of the Catholic Church, must have been the impetus for Bishop Moynagh to expel my father from the church. Again, this is purely speculation on my part as I was not privy to any of the events that transpired between my father and the Catholic Church. It was also reported by one of my siblings that our father had a fist fight with Bishop Moynagh. Again, there is no written evidence to corroborate this.

My father, Chief Akana Uyoko, was a visionary and one of the few prominent and astute minds in Mbiaya Uruan. He introduced an experimental rice farm in Mbiaya Uruan. But the venture stopped because he lacked the financial means to sustain it beyond its experimental phase. He donated some of our family land to the local government for the construction of the health center and the customary court that are still in existence today. My father became very popular among the people of our village because of his ability to heal people who were sick or afflicted by different diseases or ailments and because of his industrious effort to create wealth and employments for the Mbiaya people. The construction of the health center and the courthouse created employment opportunities for the contractors and local daily laborers.

Due to his healing power, Chief Akana Uyoko had patients and clients in Mbiaya village and in several other towns and cities in Nigeria. He used to travel a lot to faraway places within the country. Some of his travels were physical; he would be gone for weeks before returning home. Sometimes, he would travel telepathically without leaving home. It is appropriate to establish here that my father was the only man in Mbiaya Uruan to bear the name "Idio" which eventually became our family name. But where did the name "Idio" come from?

My grandmother told me that, one day, my father got into a serious trouble while he was visiting some of his patients and clients at Anang villages in Akwa Ibom State. On that day, he decided to visit a shrine named "Idio" in honor of the deity of the Anang people. The *Idio* Shrine was sacrosanct to the Anang people and it was forbidden to strangers and foreigners. On that fateful day, the chief priests of the village were performing the annual sacrifices at the holy shrine to honor their deity. It was rumored that occasionally, offerings included human sacrifices. In defiance of the deeply entrenched custom and tradition of the Anang people in that village, my father visited the shrine. Upon his arrival, the chief priests and their attendants immediately arrested him. They tied him up to a tree and left him at the shrine. The chief priests went to consult with the village head about whether to kill or sacrifice my father to appease their god. The village head agreed that it was appropriate to kill him. When the chief priests returned, they were astonished to find my father free of the ropes. My father stayed put and refused to run away to escape captivity.

The chief priests decided to tie him up again and returned to report what they had witnessed to the village head. The village head sent them back to see if my father had managed to free himself again. Sure enough, the chief priests returned for the second time to report to the village head that my father was alive and untied. A third time, the chief priest tied up my father and went back to the village chief to inform about the strange sight or occurrence. This time, the village head admonished the priests to spare my father's life should they find him untied and alive for the third time. Upon witnessing the same miracle for the third time, the chief priests were afraid and in shock because they could not explain how my father untangled the ropes and freed himself, or why he chose not to escape. They immediately apologized to him in compliance with the advice of the village head. Then, they escorted my father outside the village and set him free.

Since my father had *The Sixth and Seventh Books of Moses* with him, I am convinced that he must have invoked the appropriate magic incantations to free himself from his captivity at the Idio Shrine. When he finally returned to our village, he gathered his wives and children and told his story about his close encounter with death and his ultimate freedom from his captors. He then proclaimed to them that he was going to adopt the name "Idio" in lieu of "Udokang Akpandem Akana Udoko" as his family name to honor and celebrate his escape from captivity. And that is the origin of our family name. The name *Idio* is synonymous to whirl winds often seen during the dry season in several African countries.

My father died at the age of 45. My mother, who was very young and beautiful, refused to remain an eternal widow and married again twice. Her second husband was Ndareke from Oku Nduotong. She had my half-sister, Ini Ndarake-Ime Samuel, who died in 2003. My mother's marriage to her second husband ended 3 years after my sister Ini was born.

My mother's third husband was Etim Ibanga from Itam village. She gave him a son, whom they named Emmanuel Etim Ibanga. Her second child by the same man was stillborn due to complications. A few days after delivery of the baby by an untrained midwife (a village woman who owned a prayer house), my mother died of hemorrhage in 1962. There was no person to speak for my mother before or during the labor that led to excessive bleeding and her untimely death. I believe that if my mother had been taken to the hospital, she would have survived. The circumstances of our mother's death still haunt us all, especially my senior brother, Calixtus, who was in high school then. A few years after my mother's demise, he gained admission to the

University of Nsuka to study medicine. His regret has always been that he was not there to save our mother's life.

After my siblings and I became orphans, we were raised by our grandmother, Grandma, Adiaha Nkenta Udonya Ekpo Umoh, who died in December 1963 of a heart attack because she lost her only daughter, my mother. Grandma was industrious, strong, and wise. She raised domestic chickens, goats, and sheep in her barn a few feet from our small thatched house. On the lands that she inherited from her late husband, Udoenag Okpok Udonya Ekpo Umoh (my grandfather), she raised some crops for household consumption and traded a few vegetables and fruits to earn money to buy us clothes and school supplies. Although she had no formal education, Grandma saw in each of us the potential to become successful individuals in our chosen careers. She encouraged us to go to school to learn as much as we could. We were fortunate to inherit from our grandmother the legacy of hard work and the desire to succeed.

To me personally, Grandma was a great philosopher. I had the privilege of receiving her wise advice about strength, respect, and success. She stressed that we should be appreciative of other people who were kind to us. Early in 1962, Grandma became very sick and my aunt, Mma Nsa, took Grandma into her house and cared for her until she died. Mma Nsa was the daughter of Grandma's sister. She was married and lived in Uyo, the current capital city of Akwa Ibom State. Most days, my aunt would travel to Oron fish market to buy fish and crawfish at wholesale prices to retail in Uyo's local market. When she was away, her young children and I were left at home with Grandma. When Grandma's health deteriorated and she became bed-bound, I was always close to her and not far from her sick bed. She always advised my siblings and me to unite and support each other. While I played with my cousins in the front yards, I would go back in the house to check on Grandma in case she needed water or the bed pan.

One day, while she was still able to talk, Grandma taught me a lesson on unity and strength. To illustrate the lesson, she asked me to bring five broomsticks to her bedside. She told me to select one broomstick and break it. I broke the stick with ease. Next she told me to put two broomsticks together and then break them. I broke the sticks with some effort. She further told me to put three broomsticks together and then break them. I tried with all my might and was able to bend them, but I could not break the three sticks together. She then asked me to put all five broomsticks together and break them. That was an impossible feat for me. As a child, the whole broomsticks analogy or metaphor made no sense to me. She quickly explained the lesson of the five broomsticks. She said that the five broomsticks represented her five grandchildren: Calixtus, Lawrencia, Ini, Emmanuel, and me. That if we united and loved and supported each other, no force could break us apart. I have seen the manifestations and results of her wisdom in our lives. Although I have lost two of my siblings, the three of us who are still living have and will continue to unite, love, and support each other as long as we live. We have been more successful by living off each other's synergy.

A very uncommon event happened just before my grandma passed away. She had been bedridden for several months before her death and her ability to speak was waning fast. I was privy to the calisthenics Grandma displayed shortly before her final hours on Earth. One afternoon, after my aunt had left for Oron Market, my cousins and I were left at home to attend to Grandma. On that day, something unusual happened that I will remember for the rest of my life. After a very long silence, I heard her call me by my favorite nickname so loud and clear: "Edo-Amaowo! Edo-Amaowo! Edo-Amaowo! This nickname means (Who can love us more than God?). With joy, thinking that Grandma was getting well, I scurried as fast as my legs would take me to answer her call. For a moment, I could not believe what I saw. As I screeched to a sudden stop before my grandma, who was standing and holding both sides of the door frames, she asked me to fetch her a basket to take to the farm. The sight of her on her feet was overwhelming. Innocently and with joy, I quickly turned around to fetch a basket. But as soon as I turned my back to her, she collapsed to the floor and took her last breath. I immediately turned around to grab my grandma and I called her name, but she did not respond. I began to scream and yell as loud as my lungs could hold and my cousins rushed in to join me. We were only children with no adult to tell us what to do next. I simply removed the bed sheets and covered her body from head to toe. As we cried, one of my cousins, Sunday Iweh, ran to the nearest neighbor's house to get an adult. Luckily he met his mother who was returning from Oron Market. She moved Grandma's cold, stiff body from the floor onto the bed and tucked her in. I was told later on that sometimes when a severely sick person is about to die, he or she might do strange things (calisthenics) similar to what my grandmother did before her death. Most adults who have witnessed calisthenics would know immediately and would prepare appropriately for the ultimate end. I did not know that because I was young and naïve.

After our pillar and matriarch passed away in 1963, the three of us - Calixtus, Lawrencia, and I - were taken in by our half-sisters and half-brothers (same father, different mothers). Emmanuel and Ini, my youngest siblings from mother's other two marriages, were somewhat lucky because their fathers took care of them after the demise of our mother in 1962. The next paragraphs will describe the events that shaped my life and how my siblings and I survived it all.

1 / Intriguing Tenets

> ➤ Everybody has a story to tell.
> ➤ In some cultures, polygamy is an acceptable phenomenon.
> ➤ In some countries, a man's wealth is measured by the number of wives he marries and the number of children he has.
> ➤ Always be appreciative of other people who were kind to you.
> ➤ When you unite and love and support each other, no force could break you apart.

CHAPTER 2

The Events That Shaped My Early Life

One good turn deserves another. My father was a spiritualist. As a spiritualist, he attended to many people who sought cures and healings for different types of ailments and one of his patients was his best friend, Chief Willis Obong Eso, who came from Ifiayong Obot. My father would pray in his shrine for the divine power to bring cures and relief to his patients. Most of his patients were healed, but some died on his watch. My father tried unsuccessfully to heal Chief Eso of his disease. When Chief Eso's days were nearing their end and while he was still conscious and articulate, he asked my father for a special favor for his son, Ambassador (Amba) Willis Obong. Because Amba Willis was a good student in the primary grades, his father asked my father to train him through secondary or high school. My father promised to do so before his best friend lost his battle to his sickness.

Most of my father's children from the senior wives did not complete primary school education except a few of the sons: Eyo, Bruno, Francis, Peter, and Udofe.

Eyo attended and completed four years of secondary or high school at Aruchugwu Grammar School. He then studied as an apprentice under a master surveyor and received a certificate for surveying and draftsmanship. He established his own surveying and draftsmanship business. The surveying and draftsmanship business did not last long because he had to compete against some of the well-established surveyors and architects.

The second son, Bruno, left home and later returned as a magician. Bruno became a medicine man (native doctor) and claimed to have the power to cure diseases and ailments of all types. Bruno practiced his magic acts and became very famous. He won the hearts and minds of followers and patients who came to his shrine for cures and good luck. I also lived with him briefly. His first son died of complications following surgery in 1967 in the midst of the Nigeria-Biafra Civil War (1966-1970).

Peter, the third son whom I lived with briefly for six months, had two wives and four children. Then, his older brother Eyo (Leo) took me into his family at Uyo. Francis worked for the Federal Postal and Telecommunication Office and retired as an engineer or senior technician. Udofe was a self-trained stenographer and later became a pastor. Most of my half-sisters from the other mothers were married.

When my father lived up to the promise he had made to his friend Chief Eso to invest in Amba Willis's education, little did he know that his investment in his late friend's son's education would pave the way for Calixtus, Lawrencia, and me to excel. Late Barrister Amba Willis successfully completed secondary education and received his West African School Certificate. With that, he became a teacher. After teaching for a few years, he took a job as produce officer in the Northern Region of Nigeria and took courses that would eventually gain him admission into law school in Nigeria. While studying law, he assumed the responsibility of paying for the tuition for Calixtus to attend Holy Family College (High School) at Abak Anang. Calixtus completed his secondary school education and decided to continue his post-secondary school at a higher school level at St. Patrick College, Calabar. Calixtus was worried about Lawrencia and me. He wanted to reach out to us. He left his higher school education after a year to take a job as a produce inspector, a job Amba Willis helped him get. Calixtus took the inspector job to earn money to be able to rescue Lawrencia and me from the uncertain conditions which we were subjected to in our surrogate families.

Barrister Amba Willis paid for my primary education and Calixtus paid for my secondary education (at Holy Family College or high School, his alma mater) with additional financial support from Uncle Leo Eyo Essien, I successfully completed my secondary school education in 1973.

Next, Amba Willis took in our youngest sister, Lawrencia, and paid for her to complete primary six. Lawrencia continued her training as a grade two teacher at Teacher Training College at Ikot Ekpene. Upon completion of two years of teacher training, she became a schoolteacher until her retirement.

Barrister Amba Willis Obong took in Calixtus to fulfill the promise he made to my father - that he would sponsor any of my father's children who needed his support and demonstrated the aptitude for education through secondary school just as my father had done for him. With Barrister Willis Obong's sponsorship, Calixtus completed secondary school and went on to earn his college degree in medicine at the University of Nsuka, Nigeria. All in all, my siblings and I were the direct beneficiaries of my father's investment in his late friend's son's education.

Barrister Amba Willis Obong became our adopted brother. We have called him *Bro Amba* ever since fate brought his late father into the care of my father. I truly owe a lot to so many people who have impacted my life. Without them, I would probably not have lived long enough to become who I am today.

My Acculturation to America

I am a Nigerian by birth and an American by choice. Coming to America for the first time as a student in 1979, created in me a feeling of apprehension and excitement. In Nigeria, I grew up in the village of Ibiaku Uruan with my grandma who raised me. The farthest I had been away from Ibiaku Uruan was when I lived with my step brother, Leo at Uyo in Akwa Ibom State. Uyo is about 10 miles from Ibiaku Uruan. Back then, Uyo was not as developed as it is today. As a matter fact, the electrification of Uyo town was just beginning in the late 1960. I could still remember using kerosene lamps to light our apartment. I used lantern or candle light to do my school work.

Brother Leo and his wife Mmakon had 5 children and with me living with them, the 2 bedroom apartment was too crowded for the 7 of us in the household. At night, the furniture in the parlor were moved around to make room on the floor for straw mats for my cousins and me to sleep on. We shared domestic chores. For example, when we woke up every morning, some of us went to the public faucets to collect water. Although the taps were located about half a mile from our apartment, it usually took us about 2 hours to get water. Some mornings, we would make two trips in order to get enough water for the family. It took that long to get water because of the number of people in the neighborhood who came to the same faucets for water. Sometimes, we took turns to fill our buckets and jars. Other times, we had to fight for water. Occasionally, my cousins and I would wake up before 4:00 am to get to the water station before other people arrived. Like early birds, we would make many trips to get enough water for bathing, cooking, and for washing dishes and laundries. We did this every morning before we went to school.

As I have earlier indicated, feeding 7 people in my step brother's family at Uyo was a struggle. There were many mouths to feed, but very little food to eat. Sometimes, my cousins and I ate breakfast before going to school. We always skipped lunch. We usually ate dinner together when everybody was home. Unlike schools in America today where there are school breakfast and lunch programs for students, there was no lunch or breakfast at Presbyterian School where I attended. The breakfast that students ate at home sustained them the entire school day. Students were not bused to and from school each day. We had to walk about a mile to and from school daily. In spite of all the things that went against me, I still loved going to school. I had many friends. My teachers in grades 3-6 inspired me to work hard to be successful. Today, I am reaping a huge dividend for my hard work in school.

Like America, Nigeria was ruled by Great Britain or England until 1960 when Nigeria won its independence. The British English became the official medium of communication in Nigeria after British government granted independence to Nigeria. In Nigeria, I spoke two languages, English and Ibibio (Efik) fluently. I can write effectively in both languages as well. When I first arrived in America, I was very frustrated because I did not understand the American accent. In my college English 101class, my instructor corrected some English words that were not spelled in American way. For example: I spelled labor as labour, check as cheque, center as centre, judgment as judgement, humor as humour, honors as honours, harbor as harbour, theater as theatre, program as programme, dialog as dialogue, and many others. Once, my instructor advised, "Ignatius, if you want to pass English 101, you have to spell the words in American way." With that admonition from my English instructor, I complied and learned to spell the way Americans spell words. My accent has changed greatly, but I haven't lost that British or Nigerian accent completely. It is still detectable when I speak.

In Nigeria, my favorite snack was groundnut or Apios tuberosa (a North American climbing leguminous plant, with fragrant brown flowers and small edible underground tubers). I brought with me 2 jars of roasted groundnuts to America. The groundnuts lasted for a semester. One morning, I went to the only grocery store that was located near the college campus to buy groundnuts. My first encounter with John and Nicole Palmer, the grocery store owners went like this:

Ignatius: "Good morning Mr. Palmer!"
Mr. Palmer: "Morning Boy!"
Ignatius: "I want to buy groundnuts."

Mr. Palmer: "What you talking about boy?"
Ignatius: "I want to buy groundnuts, I repeated."
Mr. Palmer: "You want buy what Boy? I don't know what you talking about. Hey, Nicole, come and see what this boy want."
Ignatius: "Good morning Mrs. Palmer!"
Mrs. Palmer: "Morning son! What did you say?"
Ignatius: "I want to buy groundnuts."
Mrs. Palmer: "a what?"

By this time, I was totally confused and angry. I thought to myself, will I survive without groundnuts. Mrs. Palmer decided to take me around every aisle where nuts were displayed on the counters. Lo and behold! There were groundnuts in Ziploc bags and plastic jars. I could not contain my excitements after seeing different flavors of groundnuts invitingly displayed on the counters. I literally jumped to grab the biggest jar. To her amazement, Mrs. Palmer called out,

"John, come 'n here!" Mr. Palmer responded, "Boy, why didn't you say peanuts! You must be African!"

Thank heavens, my early morning encounter at the grocery store ended happily. We both learned a new name for groundnuts or peanuts. I became a regular customer at the store. John and Nicole Palmer were diligent in refilling my jar with groundnuts or peanuts to make sure I did not run out of peanuts. Looking back, I can safely say that growing up in Nigeria as a young man, prepared me for a successful life in America. Unlike Nigeria, America offered me many opportunities to earn undergraduate and graduate degrees and employment in the teaching profession. If I did not come to America, I would not have been as successful as I have become. For that, I am very grateful to be an American citizen. I hope, I have equally given back to America by teaching students in schools and in college.

2 / Intriguing Tenets

> ➤ It is true that one good turn deserves another.
> ➤ It is very fulfilling to live up to the promise you make.
> ➤ Leadership may entail ruling with big stick in one hand and a carrot in the other hand.

CHAPTER 3

Primary and Secondary Education

Ordinary people can sometimes do extraordinary things. My early education began at Peace Lutheran School, a rectangular one-building thatched structure, partitioned to house 300 pupils in grades 1-5. The school day ran from 8:00 am to 4:00 pm, Monday through Friday. I still remember learning the shapes and sounds of the alphabets and the structures and names of the Arabic numerals in grade one. We also learned to count and write the numerals 1-10 and drew the letters A-Z on our clay slates or tablets daily. We played games of tags, hopscotch, running, jumping, hula-hoop, and sang nursery rhymes. We learned to use pencils and papers in primary two. For the most part, the skills we learned in primary one continued through primary two. We also learned to add and subtract single digit numbers. We learned to use words in writing sentences in English and in our Vernacular (Efik or Ibibio). As students, we were active learners.

Primary three was a big transition for me. In primary three, we learned to think more critically, to solve mathematics story problems, and to write simple paragraphs and short stories in English and in Vernacular. We continued to play games. Soccer became very popular among the primary 3-5 students. I loved to play soccer. I started to play soccer as soon as I began to walk. At two years old, I played soccer with my diapers on.

I still remember the Headmaster, Mr. Unah and his wife. Mrs. Unah taught primary one. She made learning fun for all the children. Mrs. Unah was a great oral story teller. On mild sunny days, she always took the primary one students outside to sit under the canopy of udara tree to tell stories. I still remember the story of "The Greedy Hunter" that she told us:

There once was a greedy hunter who killed a very large elephant. With all of his energy, the hunter pulled and pulled the dead elephant, but the animal did not budge. After several attempts, he was tired and frustrated and left the elephant in the bush and ran home to the village. He asked the villagers: Please come with me to pull {*my*} elephant home. The villagers refused to go with him because he said the elephant was his. Without help from the villagers, the hunter quickly ran back to the bush and pulled and pulled the dead elephant, but the elephant was too big for him to pull by himself. The hunter ran back to the village for the second time to plead for help. But this time he said, please come and help me pull {*our*} elephant home. Immediately, the villagers scurried behind the hunter as he led the way back to his kill. Together, the villagers and the hunter grabbed the legs, the tail, the trunk, and the ears of the elephant and they pulled it with ease like a feather. As the men pulled the dead elephant closer to the village, they sang a song of joy. The women and children lined the village square to welcome the hunter and the men of the village who brought home the elephant. The men slaughtered the elephant and shared the meat with all members of the village (Mrs. Unah's Oral Folk Lore, 1958).

To me, the moral of the story of "The Greedy Hunter" is that working together makes everybody a winner.

My favorite sing-dance-act game in primary one was "Fly Like ..." and it goes like this:

Fly... like a bat
Gallop... like jungle ranger on an elephant
Hop... like a bunny
Roll... like a pumpkin
Dance... like a princess
Creep... like a cat
Walk... like a skeleton
Float... like a ghost
Stomp... like a monster
Pose like a winner (mine)

We would sing and act out the object that is named in each line. Also, the students could add their own lines and objects as I did with the *Pose like a Winner*.

At the end of the school day, some of the students walked a distance of about a mile home. Other students, who lived closer to the school, got home quicker. My grandmother was always happy to see me back home and would ask what we learned at school that day. She always prepared food for me to eat as soon as I arrived home from school. Our school did not provide breakfast or lunch for students. The breakfast we ate at home sustained us to the end of school day. My grandmother always made sure that I ate a big breakfast before leaving for school. She would say to me, "You cannot learn with an empty stomach because your stomach will be grouching the whole day." In my primary school days, we did not have the kind of testing as we do today. Teachers were very knowledgeable and astute in evaluating students to determine their levels of achievement and their readiness for promotion to the next grade level. Teachers had no problem deciding which students needed to repeat the grade. School was fun and we all loved it.

My grandmother taught me and my siblings to be honest. She said that we should not steal or take things that did not belong to us. She would say, "You cannot reap where you did not sow" (Grandma Adiaha Nkenta). She believed it was better to ask for help and assistance when we were in need than to steal. I had also read, "It's always easier to take something than work for it" (Alexandra Bracken). I think no one should be fooled into believing that a person can reap where he did not sow.

After I completed primary three, my eldest half-brother, Leo, took me away from my grandmother to live with him so I could continue the rest of my primary education at Presbyterian School in the city of Uyo. Although he had good intentions, Leo didn't have the means to support his children and me. In my brother's household, it was a struggle to have one square meal a day. His wife, Mmakon, used to sell vegetables and fruits in the local market to earn a little money to buy food for the family. My hope of continuing my primary education was almost dashed. Luckily for me, I continued primary four at Presbyterian School in Uyo. The following year, I was promoted to primary five. Mr. Effiong Bassey was my teacher. Unlike Mrs. Unah, who was a very gentle and a caring teacher, Mr. Bassey was very strict, firm, and fair. Corporal punishment was an acceptable method of discipline at Presbyterian School. It was the lashing of students that created in my mind the image of upper primary school as a place of punishment rather than a learning community. Mr. Bassey did not spare the "rod." If any students failed to turn in homework, they were lashed first thing in the morning.

Since we did not have electric light at home for me to study and complete my homework, I developed a new study habit with a few classmates who were like me. We would do our homework at school right after dismissals and turn it in first thing in the morning to avoid Mr. Bassey's whipping stick. Throughout my fifth grade year, I did not get lashed by Mr. Bassey because I was a very good student. But I did get in trouble in his class one day. I had a crush on Hannah Brown and I wanted to kiss her on the playground. Although she was my best friend in fifth grade, she objected to my offer to kiss her in front of the other students. As I tried to pull her face close to mine, I accidentally pulled on her dress and it ripped around the lapel. Boy, was I in BIG trouble! As a consequence for my misconduct, I received six lashes from the school headmaster. Ironically, Hannah pleaded with the headmaster to stop after six lashes. She later told me that she could not bear the sight of me receiving twelve strokes, which was the usual number of lashes the headmaster would administer to a student whose violation was a severe infraction of the school code of conduct. I certainly learned my lesson about kissing a girl in public.

Mr. Bassey became very interested in the ten students who demonstrated academic ability and the potential for further schooling beyond primary six. I was one of the ten students. He volunteered to tutor us in mathematics and science on Tuesday, Wednesday, and Friday morning each week. Because of Mr. Bassey's extra help in math and science, I was able to pass my primary six school leaving examinations with distinction and at the top of my class of 45 students. In my last year of primary grade, Mr. Bassey left Presbyterian School to join the Nigerian Defense Academy to train to become an army officer. He is now retired as a colonel in the Nigerian Army. The skills and knowledge that Col. Bassey imparted to me made it possible for me to excel beyond primary school. I am very happy that he came into my life as my teacher and mentor. He was very proud of me and proud of my achievements when I sent him a few presents (dress shirts, tie, etc.) in 2001.

When I thought I was not going to be able to afford the expense of completing my primary education, Brother Amba Willis, stepped in. He paid for my books and uniforms. My brother, Calixtus, who was now at Saint Patrick College, did whatever he could to support me.

He gave me his used pants and shirts so I could have a change of clothes. He arranged with his friend who owned a bookstore to let me buy books on credit.

With the support of the various people who came into my life, I got through primary school. Although I had the ambition and desire to further my education, the question was how would I afford to pay for it? There was always that inner voice within me that said, "Do not give up hope." I dreamed big because I was certain that I was destined to be successful in life in spite of the odds.

Whenever I reflected on my blessings and achievements, I honored my Creator for creating and endowing me with many privileges. I honored my father for spending his life helping others. I honored my mother for caring for me in her short span of life and for paying the ultimate price so I could live. I honored my grandmother for working tirelessly to love me unconditionally, to raise me after my mother passed away. I also honored my great grandparents for transmitting to me the gene for the "can-do spirit." I honored my teachers and mentors for scaffolding me along the path to success. All of this help and encouragement constituted a generational blessing.

Like any other child growing up, I participated in games or sports to entertain myself. My best childhood friend was Effefiong Usanga (or Da Usanga for short) – who is now a retired accountant and a pastor and still my best friend. We used to play soccer (football) together with the rest of the boys in our neighborhood. Back then, we could not afford to buy a real soccer ball. Instead, we would make our own soccer balls. We crushed several dried banana leaves together and shaped them into a sphere. After we had made a good-sized shape, we placed two or three layers of large, plane banana leaves around our self-designed soccer ball and began the painstaking steps of tying the ball with strands of palm tree fronds. We took turns weaving several strands of the fiber strings around the ball. At the end, we would have our makeshift soccer ball, with which we played on the sandy unpaved neighborhood alleys. We did not mind the fact that our hand-made soccer ball did not bounce as does a conventional soccer ball. We would play most evenings and on weekends, from morning till dusk. Luckily for us, we always played with real soccer balls at school during recess and physical education or PE.

Sometimes on weekends, we would play tournaments against our neighboring community boys with our cheering parents and other relatives as fans. Prior to the tournaments, we practiced for several hours a day. Da Usanga and I had always played on the same team. My position was offensive right-fielder. Da Usanga played the offensive center lineman. Sometimes, we won, other times, we lost. Winning or losing was not as important as the joy, the entertainment, and the satisfaction we derived from playing soccer with our friends.

Another game I used to play with my childhood friends was Nsa Isong – which boys and girls can play together. This is a board game that is often called "Mancala" in Swahili. Again, the board version was always available at schools for us to play. But at home, my grandmother could not afford the real custom-made board, so she helped me create the game pits. On our verandah, she dug six 2-inch deep pits in opposite rows for a total of 12 pits. In each pit, we put 4 marbles or small round rocks that we picked up from the local beaches. The game is played by two players. Each player grabs four marbles from a pit in his or her row and distributes them into the next pits in a clock-wise or anti-clock wise direction. The first player continues to drop the marbles or stones into the pits in both rows. As the player drops one marble at a time into each pit, the piles of marbles build up. When a player drops the last marble into an empty pit, he or she stops. Now, the other player starts to play. After each round of the game, each player will collect four marbles that are left in his or her pits. When all the pits are empty, the player with the most marbles wins the games. Nsa Isong game teaches mathematical skills such as counting and grouping numbers.

I used to participate in wrestling. My purpose for learning to wrestle was to build up my self-esteem and muscles - to keep fit and to look athletic. My appearance gained me respect from older boys and deterred the ones who might have acted aggressively towards me. After school, on most days, we would go into the bush to pick wild edible fruits and berries. Also, I used to run fast for my age. In high school, I ran the hundred-meter dash for my school in intramural sports. Growing up without parents, most of my childhood games and activities prepared me for an independent adult life.

3 / Intriguing Tenets

> ➤ Remember, ordinary people can sometimes do extraordinary things.
> ➤ Working together makes everybody a winner.
> ➤ It's always easier to take something than work for it.
> ➤ You should not be fooled into believing that a person can reap where he did not sow.
> ➤ Most of your childhood games and activities prepared you for an independent adult life.
> ➤ Childhood games and activities can prepare a person for independent adult life.

CHAPTER 4

Higher Education and Professional Accomplishments

Money alone does not determine how much knowledge a person obtains, but the desire to learn does. Setting goals in life should be a requisite for accomplishment. You see, goals can inspire you; goals can direct your talent and drive; goals can unit your followers. My quest for further study took me to the United States of America in 1979. I attended Fort Valley State University (FVSU) in Fort Valley, Georgia. I had no scholarship or loan or sponsor from Nigeria. With all my savings and a $250 gift from Uncle Leo Essien, I bought a one-way ticket on a Pan-Am flight to JFK International Airport in New York and a connecting flight to Macon, Georgia. I used the extra $1900 to buy travelers checks. I flew into New York in January and for the first time, I saw real snow. I was not prepared for snow. I had no idea how cold it would be in winter. Upon landing at the frigid airport, I was immediately advised by another passenger to buy a winter coat at the airport before I made the connecting flight to Macon. I heeded his advice and spent $80 for an oversized coat and buried myself in it. That was my first culture shock. When I finally arrived at Macon local airport at 6:00 P.M. Eastern Time, the friend who was supposed to pick me up at the airport was at work and couldn't make it to the airport until 11:00 P.M. I was hungry and tired. I had no choice but to wait for her.

Suddenly, a Good Samaritan named Paul Sanders, who, with his wife and daughter, had been passengers on the same plane, approached me. He wanted to know where I was going and if anyone was there to pick me up. I told them that I was going to Fort Valley and my friend would come for me at 11:00 P.M. Paul and his wife immediately took pity on me and decided to drive me to Fort Valley, about 30 miles from Macon. They bought me a hamburger for my dinner. When we arrived at Fort Valley, my friend was still at work and I could not get into her apartment. So, the Sanders decided to take me to the college campus. I arrived two weeks early during winter break. Fortunately for me, Mr. Palmer, the dean of students, was available to receive me and put me up in a spare room in the student union till my friend returned from work to get me. After the Sanders were certain that I was safe, they drove back home to Macon. They promised to come and visit with me on Friday. When they came back to visit, they invited me to spend the following weekend at their home in Macon. My friend, Elizabeth agreed, and I went with the Sanders for the weekend. The Sanders family consisted of the two adults and four children—two teenagers in high school and two grown children who were visiting their parents the same weekend I was there. They treated me well and I cherished and appreciated their hospitality. They were kind and caring people and became my first American friends.

My African friend, Elizabeth Ndefru, and her boyfriend allowed me to stay in their apartment for two weeks until I was able to find a roommate to share another apartment close to the college campus. I studied very hard and worked part time to pay for my college tuition and living expenses. From 1979 to 1982, I worked for Kellwood Mattress Company in Perry, Georgia, sewing the hems of the mattresses. Sewing was the only department that I was able to work in because the job was less strenuous than the quilting unit, which involved lifting, mounting, sliding, and stuffing the cottons into the steel frames. It is significant to note here that prior to my joining the sewing unit, all of the employees were females. I was the first man to break the gender line in that department. Most of my male co-employees wondered why I would choose to work in that unit. I did not mind it at all. The pay was generally good. In the summers, I picked peaches to earn additional income to support my education.

After I graduated with a Bachelor's of Arts in Economics from FVSU, I won admission for graduate study in teacher education at Grambling State University, Louisiana. I graduated with a Master's of Science in Teacher Education in 1986. I received a teaching assistant stipend that helped defray my living expenses. While doing graduate study, I took a part-time job with the Holiday Inn restaurant as a dishwasher to earn extra income.

Upon my graduation from Grambling State University in 1986, the Caddo Parish School district in Louisiana hired me to teach 5th grade at Judson Fundamental Magnet School in Shreveport. Mrs. Mary Williams was my principal. In 1989, the district decided to restructure Ingersoll Elementary School because of the poor performance of its students on the Louisiana State standardized tests. Mrs. Williams was slated to reform Ingersoll Elementary. She decided to bring along her critical mass of diligent teachers and staff from Judson Fundamental Magnet School. I was one of the teachers to accompany Mrs. Williams to Ingersoll Elementary School.

As soon as we settled down, we got the ball rolling restructuring and transforming Ingersoll. First, we revamped the curriculum. Then, we campaigned to get parents to become more actively involved in their students' education and to participate and support the effort to transform Ingersoll Elementary School. Next, we established an effective discipline program. We instituted character education activities and used them to teach the students the sort of conduct and behavior that promote strong academic performance.

Teachers volunteered to form and sponsor clubs for students to participate in after school. I formed and sponsored a soccer club for the boys and girls. We had class meetings on Wednesdays and Fridays to reflect on achievements and to plan for the following weeks. We set realistic expectations and integrated character education activities into our lesson plans and instructional methodology. We taught students to assume more responsibility for their learning. Teachers collaborated and worked as a team. Ingersoll students demonstrated their knowledge of character traits such as integrity and honesty, which are essential determinants for student success. By 1993, when I left Ingersoll Elementary, the students' performances on the state standardized tests increased from 45% to 85%. Keep in mind that Ingersoll Elementary School was among the poorest performing schools in the state, and had been designated by the district to be closed if the students' performance did not improve. I am proud to have been a part of the success story for Ingersoll Elementary School restructuring program.

In 1994, I reached a big turning point in my teaching career. I took a teaching position with the Fairfax County Public Schools district in Virginia. I taught 5th and 6th grades. That is, at Fairfax Public Schools district, the 6th Grade is middle school. I was certified to teach grades K-8. In 1996, while I was teaching at Dogwood Elementary School and Terraset Elementary School in Reston, Virginia, I gained admission to the University of Sarasota in Florida to study for my doctorate in educational leadership. It was a very challenging experience to hold a fulltime teaching position and pursue a graduate study with family obligations to fulfill. I must confess that after passing my comprehensive examination, I approached Dr. Amos Ames, who was my academic advisor, and told him that I was about to quit. That I would settle for "All But Dissertation" and a specialist degree. Dr. Ames adamantly opposed my desire to quit. He told me to rethink my intention and highlighted the benefits associated with a doctorate degree. He said, "Go ahead and proceed with your dissertation project." I heeded Dr. Ames's advice and successfully completed and defended my dissertation. In 2000, I earned my EdD degree in educational leadership. Now, looking back, I realize that if I had abandoned my doctorate, I would have regretted that decision for the rest of my life. I was driven by motivation, determination, and the "can-do spirit." I know that quitters never win and winners never quit. Now, I am deriving all the benefits of my doctorate as I continue to do what I like best, teaching and making a difference in the lives of our children. Thank Heavens that I inherited some of my forebears' tenacity, which motivated me to overcome the odds to become successful.

In 2003, I left the Fairfax County Public Schools district and joined the Michael Philip Pennington School in Prince William County Schools (PWCS). I have been teaching 4th grade ever since. Although Pennington School is a public school, it is a traditional middle school with grades 1-8. We model our school after the charter schools philosophy. Students wear uniforms, and here, too, character education has been a strong part of our school curriculum. Discipline is well managed, and students are expected to meet or exceed academic expectations. Pennington School has been designated the "School of Excellence" for many years. In 2011, I served as a co-chairperson on the School to Watch (STW) Committee. STW is a national organization that recognizes outstanding performances of middle schools in the

United States. Pennington's STW committee members worked diligently to apply for and received membership and recognition as the school to watch in 2012. Again, in 2014, we applied for and were re-designated as the school to watch in the U.S. In both instances, our STW committee members presented our project at the national conference of STW in Washington, DC, in June of 2012 and 2014. Being designated as a STW was a great honor and recognition for Pennington Traditional School, and I am proud to have been a part of this great success story. In 2010, I wrote an application for a grant to the Pennington School Parent Teacher Organization (PTO) and won the sum of $1000 to purchase the Weather Bug Station for the school. I hope to retire from Pennington School in 2020. Since no one can predict the future with certainty, I always ask my Divine Creator to grant me the wisdom to do the things I can control and the courage to accept the things that are beyond my control. In addition to my work at Pennington, in 2003, I took a part-time teaching position as an adjunct faculty at Northern Virginia Community College (NOVA) in Manassas, Virginia. I have taught integrated reading and writing courses in the department of developmental English. I have taught for 13 plus years and hope to continue to teach here at NOVA until retirement.

Jealousy and envy can sometimes breed contempt. When faced with challenges, always find a way to overcome them without being consumed. For instance, in one of the schools I taught, I was passed over for administrative position because the principal preferred a white man to a black man to be assistant principal (AP). At another school setting that I taught, the principal refused to write a letter of recommendation for me to contest for administrative position. The administrator claimed that there was nothing to write about me in spite of my exemplary teaching performances that resulted in increased students' achievement and success in the state standardized tests, every year. Keep in mind that in both situations, I was more qualified and possessed a doctorate degree in school leadership and supervision plus several years of teaching experience. I took the advice that my graduate school advisor gave me to be able to live through those challenges.

This is what Dr. Amos Aim, my graduate school academic advisor said, "If your administrator or supervisor is unwilling to recommend you for a position, do not badger, pressure, or insist because if you do, you may get a negative recommendation that may tarnish you for the rest of your professional life, especially if you are more qualified than the administrator. You have the choice to resign or change school."

My Experience Working in Nigeria

I acquired most of my working experiences in the United States. Prior to coming to the states, I worked briefly for the National Census Board (NCB) and the Federal Ministry of Labor (FML) in Lagos, Nigeria. Lagos was the first federal capital city of Nigeria. It remains still, the largest cosmopolitan and commercial city in Nigeria. Abuja is now the federal capital city.

After I graduated from high school in 1973, I was hired to work as a Data Entry Operator by the then South Eastern State of Nigeria with other 9 employees to represent the state at the National Census Board. Each of the twelve original states in Nigeria sent representatives to process the census data at the NCB in Lagos. Moving to Lagos was the first time I have been far away from my home state. Unlike living in Uyo, my state capital city, living in Lagos was very expensive. Since the job at the NCB was a temporary assignment, each employee received a fixed wage. The data operators were paid 100 Naira or about $200. The job did not provide any other benefits. The work environment was very comfortable. The data operators occupied an air-conditioned office, luxuriously furnished and equipped with computers. Food vendors catered for the workers. Although the general working condition in the data processing department was much better than in the other departments, the data operators were under constant pressure to alter the data by the states' supervisors, who were the senior officers representing their home states.

The supervisors from the Muslim Northern states did everything in their power to manipulate the census figures to favor their states by altering and inflating the numbers that were reported on the data sheets. My colleagues and I were often asked by the Northern (Muslim) States supervisors in charge of our unit to change the following census figures: 10 to 100, 100 to 1000, or 500 to 5,000. They threatened to harm us if we refused to heed their demands. We were aware of the inflated census figures, but there was nothing we could do to stop the vice. We were too naïve to report the conducts of the supervisors to the director of census. When the final result was about to be made public in 1976, General Murtala Mohammed, the then head of state of Nigeria, decided to cancel the census figures to prevent violent reactions from the citizens of the southern states of the country.

I left the NCB after one year to work at the FML as a clerical assistant for the accounting department with a starting salary of 75 Naira $150 per month. That was about 25% cut in my salary compared to 100 Naira or $200 I was paid at the NCB. I had to make drastic adjustment to adapt to the expensive living condition in Lagos. I lived with one of my half siblings in a one-bedroom apartment and shared rents. After 6 months sharing apartment with my brother, Uncle Leo Essien asked me to move in with him in his house at the federal housing estate where the senior federal employees lived. I occupied a room in the boy's quarter where his domestic servants lived, and I did not have to pay rent.

Since I did not pay rent, I began to save some money toward my undergraduate study in the United States. I started to apply to colleges in America. Fort Valley State University and Morgan State University gave me admissions. I chose to attend Fort Valley State University, Georgia. In 1978, I resigned from the FML and made final preparations to travel to the states to pursue my undergraduate education.

My immediate boss at the FML was John Enebele. John had no degree, but he was a very effective and successful bookkeeper for the department. Like me, he started his civil service career as clerical assistant and worked for several government agencies before joining the FML. He worked his way up from clerical assistant and was promoted to bookkeeper when I met him. He often smokes but John was energized when he had cigarette in his mouth and a bottle of Heineken on his desk during his bookkeeping activities. He was a very considerate person. As soon as I told him that I was planning to pursue my undergraduate study in the U.S., my boss was quick to encourage me to follow my dream. He once confided in me that he had an opportunity to attend college after graduating high school, but chose the civil service for his career instead. In addition to my education and employment achievements, I have written and published articles, poetries, and two books (see Appendix B).

➤ Money alone does not determine how much knowledge you obtains, but the desire to learn does.

➤ Setting goals in life should be the requisite for accomplishment.

➤ Goals can inspire you.

➤ Goals can direct your talent and drive.

➤ Goals can unit your followers.

➤ When you want something done, bring on board a critical mass of diligent staff.

➤ When you encounter a hopeless challenge, there is always a Good Samaritan to the rescue.

➤ Integrity and honesty are essential elements for student success.

➤ Self- motivation, determination, and the "can-do spirit" are the key to success.

➤ Tenacity can motivate a person to overcome the odds to become successful.

➤ You can always achieve your goal if you believe that quitters never win and winners never quit.

➤ Always pray for the wisdom to do the things you can control and the courage to accept the things that are beyond your control.

CHAPTER 5

Marriage and Family

Why do some marriages work and others fail? No marriage is invulnerable to problems. Every couple I know has had problems. Some couples have problems getting into marriage, while others have problems getting out of it. I believe that any man or woman who is in a marriage or entering into a marriage has to respect the other partner. Failure to do so, will cause trouble. If either or both partners won't compromise, they will have trouble. And if a couple does not share common set of values, they will also face a lot of difficulty. That being said, I believe in the significance of the union of marriage. Anybody that has not tried it, should think of doing so to experience the fun and the challenge associated with married life. I have been married twice. In both marriages, there was no long term dating prior to tying the knots.

My first wife, Mary Eugene Solomon, was introduced to me by my sister a few days before my departure for the United States. Mary was Lawrencia's friend in teacher training college at Ikot Ekpene, Akwa Ibom State. It was the norm among my people in Nigeria that any young man leaving to study abroad should marry or designate a girl whom he would marry later. My people believed that if I married a Nigerian, I would be obligated to return to Nigeria after my study.

So, within two weeks of my departure, I asked my sister, Lawrencia, to find a suitable girl for me. Lawrencia arranged for me to meet her college friend Mary the week I travelled from Lagos to Uyo to bid farewell to my siblings, uncles, cousins, and other relatives. When I met Mary, it was love at first sight…, or was it? I decided to meet her parents, Chief Eugene and Madam Inyang Solomon. The day after I met Mary, I introduced her to my older brother, Calixtus. Calixtus then took me to meet Mary's parents, bringing wine and a few items as a dowry for an initial traditional marriage consultations. That arrangement solidified into a traditional marriage contract. There was no time for background checks on me by Mary's parents or on Mary by my relatives. So, Mary was my designated wife, whom I left behind in Nigeria with the promise to bring her to the US within a year of my arrival at Fort Valley State University, Georgia.

Because of immigration protocols and procedures, it would take about 4 years before Mary could join me in the states. The American Embassy in Lagos refused to grant Mary a visa until she could show evidence that I had graduated with my bachelor's degree. As soon as I secured admission for graduate study at Grambling State University in 1983, I sent an official transcript and a copy of my BA degree in economics to Mary to take to the American Embassy for the fifth time. This time, she was granted a visa. Finally, in 1983, Mary came over to meet me at Grambling State University in Louisiana.

Life was not easy when Mary arrived. We struggled to make ends meet. Mary applied to and was admitted to study radio and television broadcasting at Grambling State University, where she was a good student. On top of everything, she was pregnant with our first baby girl, Victoria Inyang Idio, who was born in August 11, 1984. Our only income was the graduate assistant stipend of $356 I received each month. I had to take a part-time job as a busboy at Holiday Inn Restaurant on the weekends to supplement our income. In the winter of 1984, I took a day job with Reforestation Company in Ruston, Louisiana, as a member of a tree-planting crew. It was the most physically tedious and unhealthy manual labor I had ever done. The planters had to dig through frozen ice to make holes to plant seedlings. The job started around 8:00 in the morning. By noon, we were done for the day and received our pay. I remembered receiving $80 cash for that day. That was a lot of money for one day compared to the $356 monthly stipend I received as a graduate assistant. On the planting field, I was unsurprisingly the last planter to plant all my seedlings because that was my first experience. I made sure that, that first day of planting trees would be my last time to work for that company.

A few days after, I came down with pneumonia with excruciating joint and body pain and fever. We lived in a trailer home within five minutes walking distance of the campus. Mary continued to attend classes throughout her pregnancy. I was afraid she would deliver the baby in the classroom because she was way past her due date. But Mary insisted on completing her exams before she went to the hospital to deliver Victoria. She was resilient enough to make it through. The arrival of Victoria was a blessing and a burden. We were both very happy to have a beautiful baby girl, but the cost of caring for a new baby was daunting. From our meager income, we bought diapers, formula and other baby necessities. Our study time was interrupted. In spite of it all, I was able to graduate with a 4.00 GPA in 1986. After my graduation, two opportunities were presented to me.

I had the choice of continuing my doctorate study at Grambling State or accepting a teaching position with the Caddo Parish School District in Shreveport. I decided to accept the teaching position to be able to support Mary and Victoria. I left Mary and baby Victoria at Grambling so Mary could complete her degree and I visited them every weekend until Mary graduated. In Shreveport, I rented a 2-bedroom apartment with a swimming pool. With a job and a decent salary, our family life was much better than when we were students. After Mary graduated with her bachelor's degree in radio and television broadcasting in 1988, she and Victoria finally moved in and we lived as one happy family in Shreveport. That comfy, happy, nuclear family life was not going to persist for long.

Mary tried to get a job with the local television and radio networks, but none of them would hire her because she had no work permits. She was disappointed. Meanwhile, she was expecting our second child. On September 16, 1987, baby Stephanie Akon Idio was born. This time, we had the resources to raise our baby without the financial hardship we faced when Victoria was born. One would have thought that with our relatively improved and comfortable living condition in our well-furnished and well-equipped apartment, the last thing to expect would be marital problems. But as it is often said, no condition is permanent.

One day, Mary saw a strand of brown hair in the front seat of the passenger side of our car. She immediately suspected that the hair belonged to another woman, and she then accused me of cheating on her. I tried to reason with Mary, but she refused to accept my explanations. I had no reason to cheat on Mary because she was a beautiful woman, a very intelligent individual, and I loved her dearly.

I wish I knew then what I know today, I would have sought marriage counseling immediately. But we were still young and we were so full of ourselves that neither of us saw the need to work to save our marriage. Instead, I retaliated by falsely accusing Mary of her own extramarital affairs. I had no proof of her involvement with another man. It was simply baseless accusation on my part. Mary took the children and sought shelter in a home for abused women. She got a lawyer and filed for separation. After the separation hearing, arrangement was made for joint custody of the children and visitation rights were granted to me.

I tried unsuccessfully to reconcile with Mary. One day, my wife brought baby Stephanie and left her with me at the school. I had to find a substitute teacher to take over my class. Then I took the baby home. Later that day, my wife came back to our apartment to get Stephanie. Later that same evening, she returned again to the apartment to get her belongings and clothes for the children.

Help from the Immigration and Naturalization Service

An African folklore says, "A toad never crosses the highway without a reason." Following our legal separation at the Caddo Parish Family Court in 1989, Mary gained full custody of Victoria and Stephanie. I was granted visitation right on weekends: Friday, Saturday, and Sunday. The court ordered that I should return the children to Mary at 6:00 pm each Sunday. Mary, the custodial parent was ordered not to leave Shreveport with the children without my consent. Arrangement was made for child support money to be deducted from my paychecks every month and sent to Mary.

For a few months, Mary and I abided by the court decision. She dropped off the children for me to pick them up at our mutually agreed upon time and family. As my children and I were getting used to the visitation routines, one day, my lawyer told me that my wife had moved with our children to Tyler, Texas. I was very angry. I immediately thought that she could take the children back to Nigeria without my consent. My lawyer promised to arrange with her to return the children back to Shreveport so I can petition the court for full custody. But that arrangement was unsuccessful. Then, I decided to report her to the immigration and naturalization service. My rationale for taking that action was to make sure that my wife did not flee the U.S. with the children. The immigration official took information about the children and their mother and assured me that she will be monitored to prevent her from leaving the states with the children. If my wife had discussed with me prior to relocating to Tyler, Texas, I probably would not have reported her to the INS. I want Victoria and Stephanie to understand that my decision to report their mother to INS was driven by the fear that she might flee with them to Nigeria since she did not have her green card and she was not an American citizen at the time. It would have been very easy for her to buy a one-way tickets for her and for the children to travel to Nigeria. It would certainly have been dauntingly difficult for me or the INS to search, find, and retrieve my children back to the states, if Mary had decided to flee with them to Nigeria. It is important to state that I did not abandon Victoria and Stephanie. Instead, I continued to live in Shreveport, Louisiana, hoping that Mary would bring the children back. But she did not. After not seeing my children for about three years because they were no longer residing in Shreveport, I decided to move to the state of Virginia in 1994.

I take full responsibility for the collapse of my first marriage with Mary and the breakup of my family. I didn't try hard enough to make it work. I attribute the failure to the false accusations that stemmed from immaturity and selfish behavior on my part. Although Victoria, Stephanie and I have tried to have a close relationship, we are still apart from each other. I want you, my reader, to know that I provided financial support for their education in addition to paying the child support that was deducted directly from my paychecks. I am equally happy to say that in spite of the challenges that they faced, Victoria graduated with a Master's of Science degree in microbiology from the University of Houston, Texas, and Stephanie graduated with a Doctor of Jurisprudence from Florida Coastal School of Law. Both of them are successful in their professional and personal lives. I am very proud of them and I hope that they will forgive me. I want Victoria and Stephanie to have good relationship with me and their half siblings, Ignatius, Jr, and Francisca. I will always love them and I hope they will love me in return.

Like my relationship with Mary, my second marriage to Edemekong Joseph Esema came about through an introduction by a relative. While I was alone and lonely in Shreveport, Louisiana, a distant cousin, Dr. Victoria Edem, introduced me to Edemekong. Both Edemekong and I were prime candidates for a relationship. She was under tremendous pressure from her parents to get married and have children because she was the eldest daughter of a paramount chief of the Ubium Clan. Their loyalty to tradition was so profound that her relatives believed that if Edemekong should live and die without a husband or children, it would bring shame to the entire family. Since my parents died before I was old enough to be indoctrinated into the norms of Ibibio culture and tradition, I had no such pressure to get married. I had the choice to remain single for as long as I wanted because the longer I lived in America, the less constrained I was by the tenets of my Ibibio culture and tradition. But I had a more basic reason for being a prime candidate. I was lonely.

After Dr. Victoria Edem's telephone introduction in the summer of 1993, Edemekong and I became very interested in each other and willing to court each other in a long distance relationship. We spoke often on the telephone and I racked up a lot of bills. I visited Edemekong for the first time in the summer of 1993 and we were instantly in love with each other. Or were we? I made a few more trips back and forth to visit with Edemekong in Virginia. I also arranged for Edemekong to visit me in Shreveport. In Shreveport, we had lots of fun and even went on board a casino ship to play slot machines. I won $20 and with that win, I envisioned a permanent relationship with Edemekong. If I had brought an engagement ring aboard the ship, I would have proposed to her right there and then.

During my first summer visit to Edemekong in Virginia, I searched for and secured a teaching position with the Fairfax County Public Schools District. The relationship developed so fast that I could not wait to return to Shreveport to resign my teaching assignment with Caddo Parish School District and to pack up to relocate permanently to Fairfax.

In July 1994, I was fully settled in with my fiancée, Edemekong with plans to tie the knots someday. Living with Edemekong revealed a few things I did not know about her. First off, she was very upfront about telling me that she was earnestly looking for a husband because she was afraid she might die without a husband or child. She further disclosed to me that there were two other suitors whom she had hoped to marry. When she fell sick and was hospitalized with serious post-surgical complications, one of the men abandoned her before she was discharged from the hospital. The second suitor, who hailed from the same village as Edemekong, had wanted to marry her after a few years of courtship. But he broke their engagement because Edemekong's parents thought that he was not rich enough to deserve their daughter, although she was very much in love with him. So, for several years after that, Edemekong remained single. Prior to these two men, Edemekong had had a contractual marriage with an American in order to get a green card from the U.S. immigration office. She told me the stories of her experiences to test my willingness to be with her and eventually marry. I promised her that I would not behave like the other men and that I would be her husband for the rest of my life until death shall we part. That promise was kept. On May 6, 2012, Edemekong lost her battle to breast cancer.

To her credit, Edemekong was a registered nurse with a master's degree in nursing administration. She worked as a pediatric nurse at Howard University before she got a new employment with Northern Virginia Training Center to work with mentally and physically challenged patients. She was constantly sick. She had a liver disease and was a candidate on the waiting list for a liver transplant. I was afraid she might die before we got married. To make matters worse, she was fired from the Training Center. She was hired by the City of Alexandria Detox Center where she worked with recovery addicts. She was also diagnosed with breast cancer. She took disability leave and worked 3 days a week and her income was reduced by fifty percent.

In late 1994, Edemekong was pregnant with our first child. Unfortunately, the child was stillborn prematurely. In November 1995, our son, Ignatius Ini-Obong Idio, Jr., was born. On January 16, 1998, our daughter, Francisca Mfon-Obong Idio, was born. Both of our children were born prematurely, because Edemekong's poor health prevented her from carrying the babies to term. By 1996, I had started my doctorate degree program. In the midst of everything that happened to us, we decided to plan for our marriage in phases.

Phase one was the traditional wedding to be held in Ubium Village in Akwa Ibom State, Nigeria, to please and benefit the village people. A traditional wedding to the daughter of a paramount leader was a very costly venture, a little over twenty thousand dollars. First, we had to pay for air tickets to fly my parents-in-law home to meet with the elders in readiness to receive me as a future son-in-law. In January of 2000, Edemekong, Ignatius, Francisca, and I traveled to Nigeria to perform the traditional wedding. Our cost to fly to Nigeria with the children and my parents-in-law amounted to seven thousand dollars. By this time, I had completed and defended my dissertation and was ready to be graduated in June of 2000. As soon as we returned to the US after our traditional marriage, my parents-in-law came back to live with us again. They did not like to stay in Nigeria because they felt that they would not receive the same support in Nigeria as we provided to them here in the states. We had six people living in our three-bedroom townhouse. Unfortunately, my father-in-law passed away after a protracted sickness with colon cancer in 2006. Since he was a paramount leader, we had to take him back to Nigeria after we exhausted all medical treatments for him here in the States. The attending physicians decided that Chief Esema had two days to live. Immediately, we bought a ticket for him to return to Nigeria because we did not want him to die in the U.S. It would cost more money to transport his dead body to Nigeria. Two days after he arrived in Nigeria, he expired. He was buried six months after his death. Why did they delay the funeral for Chief Esema, one may ask? According to the Ibibio culture, when a reigning prominent leader dies, the body remains in state (in the mortuary) till the village chiefs decide it is the right time to bury the dead. The successor had to be appointed before my late father-in-law's body was finally entombed. The date for his burial fell during the time that schools were in session in the United States, and our children were still in school. I decided to stay and take care of them and go to work. Edemekong went home for the funeral.

My in-laws were disappointed because I did not attend my father-in-law's funeral. After the funeral, my wife returned to the states. She was still very upset with me. Our relationship became more constrained. We slept in separate rooms. Meanwhile, I felt isolated and lonely. In my loneliness and need for attention, I met and established a relationship with a mutual friend. When Edemekong discovered our relationship, she filed for divorce. By 2012, her breast cancer had spread and she received chemotherapy treatments, which made her very sick and weak. Unfortunately for Edemekong, while the divorce was still pending in Fairfax Courthouse, she lost her fight to cancer and died on May 6, 2012, without obtaining a divorce decree. It was never my intention to divorce Edemekong. The divorce proceeding stopped when she died. On that note, I can safely say that we were married till death did we part. I tried desperately to convince my in-laws to have Edemekong buried in a cemetery here in Fairfax, close to us, so that Ignatius and Francisca and I could visit her grave. But my in-laws took her body back to Nigeria for burial.

In April 2012, my wife signed three checks for the sum of $47,000 payable to my in-laws. The checks were cashed at Capital One Bank in Centreville, Virginia. In May 2012, I received the bank statement that showed the transactions. I requested my in-laws to refund $10,000 of the money to our children, Ignatius and Francisca. But my request was not honored.

Shortly before she died, my wife took off my name as the "Successor Owner" on the College fund accounts we set up for our children and replaced it with her brother's name. My children cannot collect the money without his authorization. I do not feel any remorse for severing ties with my in-laws. As President Lincoln admonished, "Stand with anybody that stands right." So, I stood with my brother-in-law when he was right, and parted with him when he went wrong. I hope he will return the college fund to Ignatius and Francisca so that they can use it to pay for their college expenses.

Perhaps, there are no simple recipes for a successful marriage. It takes a lot of quid pro quo, a willingness to give as well as to receive. Any relationship can go asunder if it is wanting in honesty, integrity, and transparency. I must also say that laughter and humor soothe and mitigate any rough edges in marriage and other relationships. In my two marriages, I have learned a great lesson about relationships. I should have provided Mary and Edemekong more affection, conversations, openness, honesty, financial support, family commitment, and unconditional love in return for companionship, felicity, beauty, support, sensual fulfillment, and unrestricted love. Women and men need these basic ingredients to build a trusting relationship.

Comparing and contrasting my two ex-wives, Mary and Edemekong, I would say this about them. Edemekong Esema Idio was very different from Mary Solomon-Idio. Edemekong was an angel. She was nonviolent. She had a genuine love for me and for our children, Ignatius, Jr. (Ini-Obong) and Francisca (Mfon-Obong). She loved her parents and siblings dearly. She was a very caring woman. As a registered nurse, she loved her patients and her colleagues. As a Salvationist, she visited nursing homes to bring food and clothes to the residents. She used to give alms to needy people. She did not like to see anybody go hungry. Left to her own discretions, she would not have filed for divorce. I think, she was misadvised and pressured by her mother and siblings to seek divorce. She was a true and loving wife to me and I loved her dearly. She took a piece of my heart with her when she died. When we took our marriage vows, I knew that we would remain married till death. And so it was.

On April 16, 2012, I had a private meeting with Edemekong, who was bedridden but conscious at St. Agnes Hospital, Columbia, Maryland. It was the last meeting before she lost consciousness. During our private meeting, we prayed for each other. She forgave me for all the wrong things I did to her and the family. I told her that I had forgiven her for any wrong things that she did to me and the family. I prayed to God to grant her peace and comfort as she prepared to die. I also said to her, "The journey you are about to take may be lonely, but you are not alone."

After that meeting, I felt very relieved but also very sad that she was going to leave us and pass on for good. To my knowledge, Edemekong did not leave any written "will" for me or for the children. Let me reiterate that it was my wish for Edemekong to be buried here in the States so that Ignatius, Jr., Francisca, and I could visit her grave to commemorate her life. However, her brothers, mother, and other relatives overruled my decision. They said that Edemekong had wished to be buried in Nigeria. May her soul find eternal peace and happiness.

At her requiem service in 2012, I read this tribute in commemoration of my dear late wife, Edemekong.

**A TRIBUTE TO MY LATE WIFE -
EDEMEKONG J. ESEMA IDIO
IN MEMORY OF HER LIFE ACHIEVEMENTS**
(June 1956- May 2012)
Date of Death: Sunday, May 6, 2012 at about
10:00 PM Eastern Time Zone (57 yrs. old).

THE JOURNEY MAY BE LONELY BUT YOU ARE NOT ALONE

As you take this lonely journey into Heaven, I want you to know that you are in the company of good friends and loved ones who will walk with your spirit in peace as you make this peaceful transition into Heaven.

While on Earth, you were a wonderful wife and mother. You were a people person. You were a team player, and a great friend. You were always generous and giving. You denied yourself so others may have. What an unselfish person you were and for that we will sorely miss you.

The trail of your goodness is endless. It will leave an indelible imprint on our minds and hearts for generations to come.

Your kindness, caring, and love for others are beacons of hope for the hopeless. Your enthusiasm and love for life was contagious. With smiles, you were always reaching out to others, especially those less fortunate.

As a Salvationist, you were an unrivalled soldier of courage and sacrifice. You were ever ready to respond to the call of duty for the goodness of God and humanity. You have made rounds and visitations to homeless and elder shelters and hospice care centers to care for the needy, the destitute, and the sick.

As a registered nurse, you have been a healer, a comforter, and a life saver.

Your life on Earth truly was fulfilling. The Almighty God who created you had plans for you. There is no doubt in my mind that you have completed your assigned mission on Earth, and God the Omnipotent Decider summons you to join the rest of God's chosen people to enjoy Eternal rest in Heavens with the Angels. And for that we can say: Halleluiah, Halleluiah, and Halleluiah,

"God is in control." When our time is up, nothing will stand in the way of the summons of God.

Your son Ignatius, your daughter Francisca, and I will continue to live your legacy. Kindly watch over and intercede for us so that we will live long enough to fulfill our missions here on Earth just like you. We love you, Dear Mother and Wife, and we will never forget you.

Your husband, Ignatius Idio - for the family.

The following e-mail is a true testament to the forgiving nature of my late wife Edemekong:

> Hi Bros: My husband and I had a long good talk last evening about the current family situation and how we have allowed it to spiral/spin out of control. It really wasn't my intention to get you into this but since my husband failed in his duty as the head of household to take control of the situation, I was left with no choice than to run to my family for help and this includes my marital family too. I reported the matter to Dr. Idio, Sr., who talked to his brother, my husband, but he kept thumbing his nose at me, which led me to act out of anger and frustration. However, after we talked to each other, he acknowledged that enough harm has been done and we (he and I) need to get back together and take care of OUR nuclear family issues without outside interference. Well, it's unfortunate that this happened, but we have agreed that this had to happen so we could learn (if there is a lesson to be learned) from it. I think now we are in a better position to talk/debate issues as mature individuals

when they come up instead of acting like kids having tantrums when we can't get our ways. So I take this chance to apologize to all of you and Dr. Idio for the trouble or heartache I/we have caused you. Hope you will forgive us and continue to pray for us and ask GOD to heal our wounds. I know my children will be happy to see us work together as a family. THANK YOU AND HAVE A VERY MERRY CHRSTMAS!!! Love always, Adia-Uka/ Edemekong Idio. (24 Dec. 2007)

Edemekong is survived by:

Daughter: Francisca Mfon Idio
Son: Ignatius Ini Obong Idio, Jr.
Husband: Dr. Ignatius Idio, Sr.

Parents:
Father: Chief Joseph Dickson Esema
(Aug. 5, 1928- Jun. 16, 2006)
Chief Esema had served in the following capacities prior to his demise: Paramount Ruler, Teacher, School Administrator, & Commissioner for Information & Cultural Affairs
For South Eastern State of Nigeria

Mother: Madam Ekanem J. Esema (April 2015)

Siblings:
Obot Esema (Late)
Ibok Joseph Esema
Barr. Essien Joseph Esema, Esq.
Sarah (Koko Mma) Joseph Esema
Esema Joseph (Obong) Esema
Udeme Esema
Aniefiok Esema

And many uncles, aunts, cousins, nephews and nieces.

In August 2012, following the passing of my late wife, the children and I attended bereavement group sessions at Capital Caring Center in Manassas, Virginia, under the directorship of Roxanne Woodward. We learned techniques we used to grieve and recover from the loss. Losing a mother took a big toll on us, especially on Ignatius and Francisca. The bereavement and grieving sessions we attended had a profound positive impact on us. I became a much stronger person, both for myself and for the children. I encouraged Ignatius and Francisca to reflect on their strengths and accomplishments and how much their mother loved them. I reminded them to remember the exciting trips they went with their mother to Nigeria, Canada, and several fun places in the States. As a result of focusing on the positive experiences and memories, they coped very well with the loss. They focused more on their school-work and made good grades in spite of their grief. I told them that their mother would be very happy to see them concentrate and do well in school.

In July 2012, I also participated in the "Parent-Teen Conflict Resolution Conference" at Piedmont Dispute Resolution Center in Warrenton, Virginia. With the knowledge and techniques that I acquired at the conference, I was able to help my children with issues and problems that they encountered after the loss of their mother. I was able to dwell less upon the loss and remained strong enough to be able to go to work. My colleagues at Pennington School were very supportive. In fact, they raised the sum of $500 for me when I told them that my wife had passed.

My children's school counselors at Centreville High School, Fairfax, Virginia, played significant roles helping Ignatius and Francisca weather the storm of disappointment, anger, and depression during their grieving. They provided regular counselling services to Ignatius and Francisca. Mrs. Jean No, the school counselor, took a special interest in my son, attending to the emotional pains and anger that he went through during the grieving process. Francisca also received counselling services from the school. These services made a big difference in how my children were able to cope with the loss of their mother. Upon graduation from Centerville High School in June 20, 2014, Ignatius (Iggy) Jr. was awarded a $600 scholarship at his graduation ceremony. He is using the scholarship at George Mason University (GMU), where he is currently an undergraduate studying applied information technology. May God bless him.

5 / Intriguing Tenets

> ➤ No marriage is invulnerable to problems.
> ➤ Some couples have problems getting into marriage, while others have problems getting out of it.
> ➤ There are no simple recipes for a successful marriage.
> ➤ Any relationship can go asunder if it is wanting in honesty, integrity, and transparency.
> ➤ A toad never crosses the highway without a reason.
> ➤ Laughter and humor can soothe and mitigate any rough edges in marriage and other relationships.
> ➤ Always stand with anybody that stands right and disunite from him when he goes wrong.
> ➤ Men and women in a relationship need affection, conversations, openness, honesty, financial support, commitment, companionship, felicity, beauty, support, sensual fulfillment, and unconditional love.

CHAPTER 6

Auto Accidents

Life is full of coincidences. There is no crystal ball with which we can predict precisely what is yet to happen. On July 1, 2014, I was attending a professional development conference at Bristow, Virginia, while my son Ignatius Ini-Obong Idio, Jr., and his four friends were traveling to Richmond from Fairfax, Virginia, to attend the Vector Marketing Company conference. I spoke with Ignatius at about 11 am and turned off my cell phone. At about 12 noon, he called and left a distressed voice mail that I listened to at 3 pm when I checked my messages:

This is the content of the distressed, nerve-racking and emotional telephone voice message Ignatius left for me on July 1, 2014, at 12 o'clock pm; "Dad, if you can hear this we have been in an accident on 95. Near Kings Dominion theme Park ... hold on ... We're trying to figure out ... if you hear this message – call me as soon as you can – Dad."

This is the frantic text message that Ignatius texted on July 1 at 12 noon: "Hey dad: If you didn't get my last msg. we were in an accident on 95. Near Kings Dominion theme pk. It was a blind spot. We are @ diner in Ashland. Near Randolph-Macon College."

The driver was seventeen-year old Khoa Pham. As he tried to merge into traffic at a very high speed, the car was hit by a delivery truck. The impact caused the car to flip over and landed on its roof in a ditch. The five occupants of the car were literally hanging upside down, strapped by their seatbelts. The police and the paramedics responded quickly, cutting open the car doors and the seat belts to free Ignatius and his friends. Miraculously, they all walked away from the terrible crash with no visible injuries. I took Ignatius to the emergency unit of Fair Oak Hospital for X-rays and CT scan to determine if there was any internal injury or bleeding. Fortunately, the X-ray and a CT scan came back negative. He had a mild concussion, and his doctor prescribed strong painkillers to relieve him of the neck pains and headache that he suffered as a result of the accident. The hospital bill was $2,500.

What a coincidence! In July 1998 at about 5 pm, I totaled my Toyota Tercel on RT 95 South near Arlington when I made a sudden exit onto a ramp at a very high speed. I hit the guardrail and the car spun around and faced the opposite direction. I was driving back from Florida that day after completing my graduate course work for the semester at the University of Sarasota. Although my car was damaged beyond repair, I walked away with only a mild concussion. Because Ignatius and I both walked away from our very serious car crashes essentially unharmed, I had to accept the simple truth that there was a higher power who was in control of the accidents and the outcomes. With that conviction, I will eternally remain grateful to the Divine Order that protected us and spared our lives.

6 | Intriguing Tenets

> ➤ Life is full of coincidences.
> ➤ There is no crystal ball with which we can predict precisely what is yet to happen.
> ➤ There is always a higher power who watches over us.
> ➤ Be Grateful to the Divine Order that is omniscient and in control.

CHAPTER 7

World Events and Political Party Affiliation

In 1966-1970, the Nigerian Civil War (aka Biafran War) was fought because of the unilateral secession of the Eastern Region, Nigeria, from the rest of the country. The war began after a failed attempt to negotiate peace at Aburi, Ghana, between General Yakubu Gowon, the military head of state of Nigeria, and Colonel Chukwuemeka Odumekwu Ojukwu, the leader of Biafra. Colonel Ojukwu was appointed the military administrator of the Eastern Region, Nigeria, in 1967, shortly after the 1966 military coup that seized power from the Federal Republic of Nigeria. While it is true that the secession received widespread support among the Igbos of the Eastern Region, the minority tribes of the Eastern Region did not favor the separation because of fears that the Igbos would dominate them. Looking back, I was very fortunate to survive the civil war. I lost quite a few friends in the conflict. I was eager to join the army on the side of the Biafran rebels, but I was too young to be drafted.

Every individual is entitled to life, liberty, and happiness. I am a registered voter and a Republican since becoming a U.S. citizen in 2001. In the 2008 and 2012 presidential elections, I crossed the party line and voted for President Obama. It is obvious that I voted that way because I am an African American and I wanted to vote for a black president when the opportunity presented itself. I was not sure I would have another opportunity to vote for a black man for president of the U.S. If a woman runs for president, I will surely vote for her, irrespective of her party affiliation. I still believe that most female presidents would be more reluctant to go to war than their male counterparts.

As a U.S. citizen, I cherish the freedom to participate and exercise my right to vote in local, state, and national elections. I appreciate the opportunity to participate fully in the democratic process because of the sacrifices the civil rights leaders made to pave the way for African Americans and other minority groups to have the right and freedom to vote. That in itself is a blessing. The present and future discharge of my civil duties and responsibilities will rest upon the tenets of the Declaration of Independence, beginning with the eternal pronunciamento or proclamation: "We hold these truths to be self-evident; that all men are created equal; that they are endowed by their Creator with certain inalienable rights; that among these are life, liberty, and the pursuit of happiness."

I must acknowledge the struggles and sacrifices that Dr. Martin Luther King, Jr., Rosa Park and other civil rights fighters made on my behalf and the behalf of all African Americans and other minority groups. The struggle to achieve full equality for all Americans continues today. We, the American citizens, must continue to build upon the legacy of the freedom-loving civil rights leaders who paved the way for "Liberty and Justice for All." America has the power, the resources, and the technology to make the world a better place by investing in programs that will foster peace beyond our shores.

The 16th president of the United Sates, Abraham Lincoln (a Republican, 1860-1865), is and will continue to be my hero because he stood firmly and believed that the principle of the Declaration of Independence included all men and women. He supported the voting rights for black Americans; he stood against the other interpretations of the doctrine of the Declaration of Independence, such as those declared by the slave owners and masters. "For some men to enslave others is a sacred right of self-government" (Lehrman, 2013). I admire Lincoln's resoluteness in deciding to fight the American Civil War to maintain the Union and abolish slavery. Lincoln was a self-made American and a hard working citizen who taught himself little by little to become a prominent lawyer and politician. Nowhere has it been documented that President Abraham Lincoln owned slaves. He was the champion of civil rights for all minority groups in America. President Abraham Lincoln was a man who was light years ahead of his time.

I have grown to admire the following leaders of the 20th and 21st centuries because of their political aspirations and philosophies, their views on the global issues, their struggles and sacrifices for human rights, and their leadership:

1. Sir Abubakar Tafawa Balewa: The 1st Federal Prime Minister of Nigeria
2. General Murtala Ramat Mohammed: head of the Military Government of Nigeria
3. Chukwuemeka Adumegwu Ojukwu: the rebel leader of the defunct Biafra
4. Mohandas Karamchand Gandhi: the preeminent leader of India who employed nonviolent civil disobedience to win freedom from Great Britain for the people of India

5. Indira Gandhi: Prime Minister of India until her assassination in 1984
6. Ellen Johnson Sirleaf: the 24th and the first female President of Liberia
7. Nelson Rolihlahla Mandela: the 1st Black President of South Africa
8. Dr. Martin Luther King, Jr.: American Civil Rights Leader
9. Ronald Reagan: the 40th President of the United States
10. Bill Jefferson Clinton: the 42nd President of the United States
11. George W. Bush: the 43rd President of the United States
12. Barack H. Obama: the 44th President of the United States
13. Archbishop Emeritus Mpilo Desmond Tutu of South Africa

Some of these men and women who have impacted my generation, have demonstrated elements of conservatism in their leadership styles, and others have favored liberal ideas. Most importantly, they were, in my opinion, pragmatic leaders who strived to encourage global peace, to inspire the movements for civil rights and freedom, and to eliminate human suffering across the world during their tenures in office.

Still, I have come to believe that no country can in isolation, guarantee national security for its citizens. President Barack Obama stated it succinctly in his book, *The Audacity of Hope,* "Like it or not, if we want to make America more secure, we are going to have to help make the world more secure" (Obama, 2006).

We are now members of one global community and we have to transform our thinking from the age-old perception that each country can survive independent of the rest of the world, irrespective of its standing in global society. Human beings are by nature social animals and with the inception of technological advancements and global interconnectivity, we cannot hide behind or be confined within our national boundaries. We have to collaborate with other nations even if they do not embrace our particular political philosophy and beliefs. We must learn to get along and cohabit the earth peacefully.

In his view of the world in which we now live, President Obama warned us that:

> In the past, there was the perception that America could perhaps safely ignore nations and individuals in these disconnected regions. They might be hostile to our world views, nationalize a U.S. business, cause a spike in commodity prices, fall into the Soviet or Communist Chinese orbit, or even attack U.S. embassies or military personnel overseas – but they could not strike us where we live. September 11 showed that's not the case. (2006)

The world is ever-changing and we should not remain stagnant. We should all play active roles in our changing world. Before I take my leave of the world someday, I would like to witness a permanent ceasefire between the people of Israel and the people of Palestine. As a democracy and the more industrialized country in the West Bank and Gaza region, the Israelis should take the initiative to reach out to their Palestinian neighbors to help rebuild their infrastructure, develop employment opportunities, and dismantle the walls that divide their lands so that the two nations can live in peace and harmony. On the other hand, the Palestinians must recognize the right of the Israelis to live side by side with them in the West Bank and Gaza.

We have to come to the realization that the Israeli and Palestinian conflict will never be resolved by the American people or by any other country – only by the people of Israel and Palestine. Peace and tranquility will not return to West Bank and Gaza by vicious cycles of fighting, but by genuine negotiations between the two peoples. The rest of the nations should provide the necessary resources to support the rebuilding of conflict-riddled Palestine. There will be no peace in Israel or Palestine if the Palestinians are hungry. There will be no peace in Israel or Palestine if the Palestinians' homes and businesses are demolished or if the occupation of the Palestinian's lands by the Israelis persists. However, I believe that by giving peace and freedom to the Palestinians, the Israelis will secure permanent peace and freedom for themselves.

When the Palestinians are gainfully employed and living productive lives, they will not have the time to worry about making crude rockets to launch at Israel or digging tunnels to get to Israel. If required to for self-defense, Israel would always respond with missiles to kill the Palestinians and destroy their homes, businesses, and infrastructure. Palestinian fighters will always lose to the sophisticated Israelis army. In the fighting between the Israelis and Palestinian Hamas from July 8th through August 2014, nearly 2000 Palestinians, including Hamas fighters, died. About 85% of the deaths were civilians including children and women. In contrast, fewer than 100 Israelis soldiers died, with about four civilians. In my opinion, the war was very one-sided because the rockets that Hamas fired into Israel were no match for the deadly missiles and bombs that the Israel armies fired against Palestinian homes, businesses, United Nations schools (used as shelters for Palestinian refugees), and hospitals. I think the Israelis soldiers should be indicted for war crimes for attacking the hospitals and killing men, women, and children. The longer the conflict between Israel and the Palestinian lasts, the less likely the chance for peaceful cohabitation between the Israelis and the Palestinians.

After more than two decades of fighting between Israel and Palestine, I can only surmise that the Israelis and the Palestinians cannot survive as half-victors and half-victims for much longer. Both sides need a strong conscious adjustment to break the vicious cycle of war that only deprives them of life, liberty, and the pursuit of joy. Israel must lift the blockade to let Palestinians move freely and stop the settlement of Palestinian lands. The Palestinians must recognize the right of the Israelis to exist and stop building tunnels to Israel. Both sides must lay down their arms because "he who lives by the sword will perish by the sword." If they perpetuate the conflict, it will someday dawn on the Israelis and the Palestinians that they have depleted a generation of youth who would have become future leaders of both nations.

After several years of war between Israel and Palestine, any chance for peace will come at a terrible cost. Before a permanent peace is achieved, the citizens of both sides will be killed. Before a permanent peace is achieved, the citizens from both sides will be abducted and imprisoned, and before a permanent peace is secured, the homes, businesses, and infrastructure in Israel and Palestine will be destroyed. But if this is the price the Israelis and the Palestinians have to pay to attain a permanent peace, to live side by side and exonerate their children from psychological destruction, then nothing could be more honorable.

In 2005, I wrote and published the following poem and dedicated it to the children of Israel and Palestine:

BEFORE MY JOURNEY ENDS

Before my dream fails
Will the children of Palestine and Israel

Jointly rebuild their two states
From the rubbles of decade ruins
To insure progress for generations to come?

Before my hope fades
Will the children of Palestine and Israel
Hold hands like Guardian Angels
And Walk across Jerusalem and Bethlehem
In peace, love and brotherhood?

Before my faith wilts
Will the children of Palestine and Israel
Work, play and dine together
And enjoy the fruits of their labor
In peace, love and happiness?

Before my journey ends
Will the children of Palestine and Israel
Live for the first time and forever
In harmony with all and hatred for none
To let freedom ring from East to West Jerusalem?

The Answers I Predict, Rest With The
Leaders Of The Free World.
(Idio, 2005)

The sooner the people of Israel and Palestine understand the nature of the three social evils, namely, "the evil of war, the evil of economic injustice, and the evil of intolerance," the greater the likelihood that these perpetual belligerent neighbors will be able to cohabit their lands peacefully. Dr. Martin Luther King, Jr., once said, "War stacks our nation with national debts higher than mountains of gold; war fills our nations with orphans and widows; war sends men home psychologically deranged and physically handicapped" (Honey, 1963).

More often than not, the evil of economic injustice creates wealth for the rich and brings abject poverty to the poor citizens of that region. The evil of intolerance prompts the Israelis to create a blockade against the Palestinians to prevent the free movements of persons, goods, and services across both sides. It further creates unemployment and discrimination among the Palestinians. The evil of war, the evil of economic injustice, and the evil of intolerance are created by people and it is the people who have to work together to overcome them.

I think that the sooner we believe that we are as much alike as human beings as we are different, the larger the opportunity for us all to live together in peace and harmony. Whether we are gay, straight, black, white, Muslim, Christian, Jewish, Buddhist, atheist, or agnostic, the natural truth is that we have a similar beginning – birth – and a similar end – death, which none of us will escape. We should invest in people and build a thriving community of people to love and to be loved because during our life journeys and at the end of our lives, we need others to survive. Since a tree cannot make a forest, a person cannot make a nation.

> ➤ Every individual is entitled to life, liberty, and happiness.
> ➤ Most female presidents would be more reluctant to go to war than their male counterparts.
> ➤ For any citizen to have the right and freedom to vote is in itself a blessing.
> ➤ America has the power, the resources, and the technology to make the world a better place.
> ➤ The principle of the Declaration of Independence included all men and women.
> ➤ No country can in isolation, guarantee national security for its citizens.
> ➤ The world is ever-changing and we should not remain stagnant.
> ➤ Vicious cycles of war only deprive us of life, liberty, and the pursuit of joy.
> ➤ Naturally, we have a similar beginning – birth – and a similar end – death, from which no one will escape.

CHAPTER 8

My Wishes and Words of Encouragement

It is better to establish your wishes while you are alive than to have someone else make them for you after your demise. Here is my simple wish. I wish that all of my children will be successful, independent, and established by the time I am ready to take the ultimate bow to my creator's order to move on. I also wish for the family name *"Idio"* to be sustained as an eternal legacy from generation to generation of my posterity.

As a human being, my greatest apprehension and vulnerability as I prepare to embrace the journey into the afterlife is a fear of protracted, tormenting, and debilitating health issues such as cancer, Alzheimer's, amyotrophic lateral sclerosis (ALS) or Lou Gehrig's, dementia, Parkinson, and diabetes. On the other hand, if I could dictate how I want to die, I would choose to feel healthy and happy and have a smile on my face in the days leading to my expiration. My end should be celebrated with joy rather than with grief and sorrow. Because I have no regrets for the life I lived, I can conclude with certainty that I have been one of the fortunate creatures to have lived on the face of the earth. Beyond my concern for my children, my greatest wish is that since the earth is and will continue to be our only permanent habitat that sustains life, we do everything in our power to preserve, conserve, and safeguard the resources in the ecosystem for the current and future generations.

My experience in life has taught me well enough that I can debunk the old myths that because of our racial, ethnic, and religious differences, we are not the same inside. In spite of our varied natural endowments and attributes, we are similar creatures from a common ancestry (Homo sapiens) and therefore, we all deserve fairness. That is how we should treat our fellow human beings. We all deserve respect and love. The world will be a much better place if we respect and love one another.

Laughter, happiness, humor are indispensable for longevity. Laughter is the best therapy. I smile and laugh a lot. I exhibit a sense of humor. As an educator, having a sense of humor has kept me sane and healthy. If you want to live a long healthy life, you have to laugh a lot and display a good sense of humor. The senior pastor of Lakewood Church in Houston, Texas, once said, "A friend of mine had a good-humored grandmother who lived to be 103 years old. When she went into the hospital at the age of 100, my friend called and asked her what was wrong?" The grandmother answered, "Well, so far they ruled out pregnancy."

A good hearty laugh can keep a person young at heart. Even if it is simply laughing over a shared memory with a close friend, watching a movie, reading a book, or forcing a laugh to ward off a bad mood, the benefits are overwhelming. A good laugh can foster a positive attitude and keep you in a happier state of mind. In their "Laughter and Antiaging" article, a group of endocrinologists advised that laughing uses a lot of muscles, arouses the immune system and stimulates our minds. Their research study showed that "only 30% of longevity is genetic and 70% you control with your mind on how you think, with your body on how you keep yourself in shape, and the lifestyle you choose to live" (Laughter and Anti-aging). The anti-aging medical doctors or anti-aging

MDs further identified the following as the "anti-aging reasons" to laugh daily:

- It reduces stress
- It is a natural anti-aging tool
- It helps us sleep better
- It improves lung capacity and blood oxygen levels
- It is contagious - it will extend to the people around you (anti-aging MDs)

At age 10, my son, Ignatius Jr., made a similar point about the impact of laughing on good health and longevity. He advised his mother and me to laugh daily in order to stay healthy, to enjoy life and to live longer. Boy, was Ignatius right there on the money! The 2012, Longevity Genes Project, an Albert Einstein College of Medicine study conducted on the centenarians of Ashkenazi (Eastern European Jewish descent) concluded, "optimism, laughter may bring long life" ("Longevity Genes Project," 2012).

About the same time period, a team of scientists led by Dr. Thomas Perls, director of the New England Centenarian Study at Boston University Medical Center, reported that the findings of the "Longevity Genes Project" confirmed several observations he and his colleagues have made in the past. Dr. Perls and his research team looked uniquely at personality traits typically found among the children of centenarians and found the children to be high in neuroticism and tended to dwell on things and internalized their stress rather than let it go. The researchers noted that that behavior "can translate into increased risk for cardiovascular disease." (Perls, reported: 2012).

In my lifetime here on Earth, I have lived a fulfilled life full of joy, happiness, and humility. I have always been humbled by the experience of living. Because my parents died so young, I wanted more than anything else to be able to trump the odds and live longer than my parents. Now, I believe that I can make it beyond the age of 70, although I understand that when my time comes and my Creator summons me to exit the stage, I must yield to the order. Remember, we are but actors on Earth and we have our entrances (births) and exits (deaths). Another thing we have to internalize is that we all came into this world bare and we will return bare. When our time arrives for the final passage, we will take none of our earthly riches and wealth to our eternal destinations.

No matter how much money we possess, it cannot substitute for the things that really matter in life. For example, can we substitute money for tenderness? Can we substitute money for love? Can we substitute money for gentleness? Sometimes, we use money as a status symbol to show off our wealth and power. I once read, "If you're trying to show off for people at the top, forget it. They will look down at you anyhow. And if you're trying to show off for people at the bottom, forget it. They will only envy you" (Albom, 1997). In the final days of my life, it will not matter whether I was rich or poor. What will matter is the number of people I touched and whose lives I made a difference in while I was alive.

I am blessed to have lived and witnessed the evolution of information technology. We should use technology to enhance the preservation of lives on Earth. It doesn't matter who we are at a given moment and time; it doesn't matter what orientation we come from; but what really matters the most is that we need each other to survive in our ecological environment. That is, all human beings must cohabit interdependently with the rest of the species in the ecosystem.

I smile a lot and try to make laughter a lifetime habit. Laughter has the power to "heal your body, soothe your spirits, attract admirers, and mend your relationship" (Osteen, 2010). It is equally important to share one's knowledge and wisdom. My grandmother once explained to me that when you learn something new and teach it to many people, your knowledge about the thing you learned continues to increase exponentially.

Also, there is no greater legacy than to help another person succeed. I have read, "When you do for others what they cannot do for themselves, you will never lack God's favor. You will never lack God's blessing" (Osteen 2010).

There is no justification for war, although some politicians and war hawks may think otherwise. Whether we are fighting a civil war, bilateral war, international war, or world war (as in World War I and World War II), there are never any clear victors. Instead, both parties always suffer in terms of human and property casualties. That is why I think we should avoid war altogether and at all costs. Can we imagine a world without wars? The choice belongs to the future generations.

Although I appreciate kind and encouraging words from people around me, I often remained unfazed by negative vibes from those who talk down to me. Here, I refer to those people who thought I would not amount to anything in life. I think self-encouragement was the motivator that propelled me to greater heights. There were times when I was discouraged and ready to give up. For instance, when I grew up without parents, when I went for some days without food, when I thought I was not going to be able to pay for my education, or when my marriages were unsuccessful, then self-encouragement sustained me. Instead of dwelling in self-pity, I would turn to my "can-do" spirit. I refused to quit in times of challenge and hopelessness. I always tell myself that I am strong, talented, and that my best is yet to come. I always celebrate my successes and achievements without being arrogant.

Like Osteen (2010), I believe strongly that "Every setback is a set up for a comeback."

I also like to do several things to stay emotionally, mentally, and physically balanced. I like romance, but I do it in moderation. I like all types of food, but I eat them in moderation; and I like to drink wine and beverages, but I drink them in moderation. I realize that all of my indulgences have been done in moderation and that habit has been the formula for my good health. People often ponder the question, is anything possible in life? My response is simple. If you have Divine Providence in the equation, the answer is "yes."

8 / Intriguing Tenets

- ➢ It is better to establish your wishes while you are alive than to have someone else make them for you after your demise.
- ➢ In spite of our varied natural endowments and attributes, we are similar creatures from a common ancestry (Homo sapiens).
- ➢ The world will be a much better place if we respect and love one another.
- ➢ Laughter, happiness, humor are indispensable for longevity.
- ➢ No matter how much money we possess, it cannot substitute for the things that really matter in life.
- ➢ Laughter can heal your body, soothe your spirits, attract admirers, and mend your relationship.
- ➢ There is no greater legacy than to help another person succeed.
- ➢ There is no justification for war, although some politicians and war hawks may think otherwise.
- ➢ Do not dwell in self-pity, turn to your "can-do" spirit.
- ➢ If your indulgences are done in moderation, they can be a formula for good health.
- ➢ Use technology to enhance the preservation of lives on Earth.

CHAPTER 9

My Optimum Rewards

Everyone likes compliments. Educators have not been accorded the rewards that they rightly deserve. If I had my ways, teachers would be the highest paid professionals in every country of the world because they have the power to change life one student at a time. None of our professionals and leaders, including presidents, scientists, astronauts, medical doctors, accountants, business gurus, lawyers, programmers, and technologists, would have attained their current status if they were not taught by teachers. I know and believe that all educators value the simple acts of appreciation that come from students, parents, and members of the school community.

The Catholic Church Holy Father, Pope Francis expressed similar sentiment when he said:

> Teaching is a beautiful profession. It's a pity teachers are badly paid, because it is not just about the time they spend in school, but the time they spend on each individual student. I think of my own country [Argentina], where many teachers have to work double shifts just to be able to get a decent wage. But what state will a teacher be in after a double

shift? (June 2015)

I am very fortunate to have been handsomely rewarded by many of my students and their parents, who have shown how much they appreciate me as a teacher who made a positive difference in the lives of their children.

The following examples include testaments, compliments, and appreciation from some of my students and their parents. These invaluable notes are the most treasured blessings and rewards that I have earned during my teaching career. They affirm my decision to take up teaching as a lifetime profession. They are worth more than material things I have acquired over the years. I can speak on behalf of all past, current, and future teachers and educators around the world because I know deep in my core that we, as professionals, place a high premium on students' and parents' compliments because those gestures validate what we do for each child every day. Teachers truly make a positive difference in the life of a child and in our society as a whole. I am the beneficiary of the time and effort that my teachers have invested in me. I am delighted to share these priceless treasures with you, the reader.

June 11, 2015
E-MAIL& CARD from Mr. and Mrs. Cameswara Rao Sista (Parents of Adhbuth, my 2014-2015 4th student)

On behalf our family, please accept our heartfelt thanks for your hard work, diligence, consistent care you provided to Adhbuth Sista and in general to every 4th grader in your class.

Your communication is consistent, teaching style a mixture of intellect, setting priorities, healthy humor suits many young kids.

Be assured Adhbuth and us will remember the foundation you laid for him and build on it over the years to come.

Thank God for eminent and dedicated educators like you.
We dedicate all his awards to your sincere and honest coaching and mentoring.

Best wishes for your future. If we can be of any assistance for you ever, do not hesitate to contact me.
Kameswara Rao Sista (SK)-Adhbuth's Dad
Challuri Radha Kumari (Mom)
Deevena Sista (Sister)

Card made and given to me as a present by my student
(June 11, 2015)

9 / Intriguing Tenets

➢ Everyone likes compliments.

➢ Teachers should be the highest paid professionals in every country of the world, why?

➢ None of our professionals and leaders, would have attained their current status if they were not taught by teachers.

➢ Educators value the simple acts of appreciation that come from students, parents, and members of the school community.

➢ An effective teaching style mixed with intellect, setting priorities, and healthy humor often suits many young kids.

CHAPTER 10

Life is Transient

The way we enter the world, so shall we exit. It is true that each person arrives at birth bare and naked. At death, we will take nothing with us. Having said that, why, I must ask, do we cling so firmly to material things? Money, wealth, and power will not stop us from dying. None of them will follow us beyond the Earth. Money, wealth, and power are not substitutes for tenderness, gentleness, and friendliness. When we put our values in the wrong things, we end up with very disillusioned and unfulfilled lives. I see life in any form as a transient experience. Everything associated with life is impermanent. It is important to learn how to die in order to learn how to live. Because we are so ambitious to acquire material things by any means possible, we often lose sight of the meaning of life as it relates to death. If I had the option to decide how I want to die, I would simply say, I want to die placidly and tranquilly. I know, when my time comes, I will return to my Creator bare and naked just as I came into this world. I hope by sharing my feelings in this poem, I can help you to understand death in order to understand life.

Things That Matter the Most

The first of these is life.
Life is what we do every day.
Life is the only juggling act.
It's a bridge between living and dying.

Following life is love.
Love overcomes fear.
Love builds trust.
It cultivates respect too.

Next to love is compassion.
Compassion brings empathy.
Compassion brings sympathy.
It brings kindness too.

Death is the referee of life.
Death guides our path through life.
Death whistles when we falter along the way.
It decides if we're winners or losers too.
Life, love, and compassion are the things that matter the most.

How I Want to Be Remembered

Readers of this memoir, please remember me by these simple words: *I came. I lived. I learned. I served. I made a difference.* If there is another life to live beyond the one I spent on Earth, then I would like to be and live like a frog (amphibian). Why? Frogs live both in water and on land. My desire to be and live like a frog should not be questioned because that is simply me. You have the right to differ from it.

As mortals, we should not be afraid of death because death is as natural as life. It is part of the pact we made with our Creator.

We are part of nature. Everything that is born will die. Some of the most important things in life are love, responsibility, spirituality, and awareness. Death only ends life, not love or relationships. Each of us should love and take responsibility for one another. Since there is no formula for a successful relationship, we have to negotiate in tender ways, giving both partners the chance to express their wants and needs, and their hopes for what they can accomplish with their lives. We should be aware of the beauty of nature, of the plants and animals that are members of the ecosystem to which we belong, and treat them as our codependent species. We should exercise spirituality by communicating with our Creator. Above all else, we should make peace with ourselves and everyone else around us. We should forgive ourselves and others before we take the last breath. If we wait, we may not get a chance to forgive, and we will exit the Earth with our souls carrying the heavy burdens of guilt.

10 / Intriguing Tenets

> ➤ The way we enter the world, so shall we exit.
> ➤ Don't be afraid of death because death is as natural as life.
> ➤ You are part of nature.
> ➤ At death, we will take nothing with us.
> ➤ Money, wealth, and power will not stop us from dying.
> ➤ Everything associated with life is impermanent.
> ➤ Life is a bridge between living and dying.
> ➤ Death is as natural as life.
> ➤ We should forgive ourselves and others before we take the last breath.
> ➤ Remember, all lives intersect.
> ➤ Sharing and service to others constitute the ultimate joy and happiness.
> ➤ Remember, even strangers are family you are yet to get to know.
> ➤ Life means creating something that brings you purpose and meaning.
> ➤ Life also means devoting yourself to loving people in your community.
> ➤ Finally, life means leaving a permanent positive imprint on the sands of time.

FINALE

It may happen that the setting at the end of my life is not similar to the setting at the beginning. Wherever the setting might be for my final days, I will be completely and totally willing to accept the hand of destiny without reservation. Life and death are the two extremes that every human being has to experience. I do not believe in life after death, as do so many people. People of different religions espouse the belief that "Jesus the Son of God" rose from death after three days of interment. Only Jesus had the power to rise from death. I do not believe that my parents and grandparents are alive somewhere. If it were possible for the rest of us to live or reincarnate after death, my parents would have returned to visit me and my siblings. The conviction that they are not alive and will never return is the foundation of my rejection of the phenomenon of life after death. My belief should not in any way infringe upon the liberty of the rest of you, who might want to believe otherwise. When I die, that will be it for me. In other words, I was born, I lived, and I died. That is, the beginning, the middle, and the end of me and nothing else.

However, I strongly believe that all lives intersect. I read somewhere that death does not "Just take someone, it misses someone else, and in the small distance between being taken

87

and being missed, lives are changed." And even "strangers are family you are yet to know (Albom, 2003). That being the case, we should all respect one another. We should seek forgiveness when we encroach upon the rights of others. We should do everything possible to cohabit the Earth peacefully as one global family. Therefore, my apologies to those people whom I might have offended or violated by my dealings, actions, interactions, and relationships with them. Their unconditional pardons will be eternally appreciated.

To me, sharing and service to others constitute the ultimate joy and happiness. The Associate Justice of the Unites States Supreme Court, Sonia Sotomayor, said it best in an interview with Daryl Chen of *Reader's Digest* in 2014, when she was asked, "What is your idea of happiness?" Justice Sotomayor responded, "I think it would be the satisfaction of enjoying things with others – meaning when you are giving to others, whether it is time, attention, a gift, or anything. Just those moments of sharing" (Chen, 2014).

Some people consider money to be the most important thing in life. I have been weighing this perception about money. I have come to the conclusion that forming connections to the citizens of our global society will make us happier than having tons of money. Don't get me wrong. Money is a necessary resource, but it should be used to meet our individual needs. Keep in mind, no one has taken and none of us will take money or wealth with us when we reach the end of our life on Earth. Share your knowledge and be generous with extra resources and wealth in your possession while you are alive. People will remember your generosity more than anything else you leave behind.

I have often been asked the question, *what is the meaning of life?* Life to me means creating something that brings you purpose and meaning. Life also means devoting yourself to loving people in your community. Finally, life means leaving a permanent positive imprint on the sands of time.

My parents, grandparents, and great grandparents were extremely adept and diligent at showing and sharing love. They gave it all to me and my siblings for us to live and be successful. The only regret I have about the intriguing journey of my life is that while my parents and grandparents gave me everything, they died before I had a chance to give them anything in return. At the end of a life journey, it becomes evident that we aren't as we began.

ACKNOWLEDGMENTS

The Intriguing Journey of My Life would not have been accomplished without the astonishing support of the following people.

My grandmother (Grandma), Adiaha Nkenta for being the pillar and the source of my strength. She raised me, loved me unconditionally, and encouraged me to dream big and pursue my dreams.

My mother, Akon for her love for me and for making the ultimate sacrifice when she died very young.

My father, Francis, for his generosity and kindness and willingness to assist people.

Mary Solomon-Idio, my ex-wife for the opportunity for me to look back at my life experiences with her.

Ma Edemekong Esema Idio, my second and late wife for her love for me and our children and for forgiving me of my missteps before she departed this world to eternal rest.

Ignatius, Jr. and Francisca for editing the initial drafts of my story. They provided the extra eyes to catch typos, usage, and sentence errors that eluded me.

Victoria, my first daughter, for editing and proofreading the manuscript to correct any mistakes that might have escaped me or my editor.

Margaret, my editor, for her attention to details in correcting the manuscript. She suggested that I needed to include a story about my acculturation to America and my working experience in Nigeria. To each of these people, I owe a great deal of gratitude and appreciation.

REFERENCES

Adiaha, Nkenta. (1952-62). Grandma's Life Lessons & Philosophies.

Albom, Mitch. (2003). *The Five People You Meet in Heaven.* New York: Hyperion. Print.

Albom, Mitch. (1997). *Tuesdays with Morrie.* New York: Broadway Books. Print.

Archdiocese of Calabar. (1947). "Historical Summary." < http://www.catholic-hierarchy.org/diocese/dclbr.html> Web. 3 Aug. 2014.

Barzilai, Nir. (2012). Longevity genes project. *Albert Einstein College of Medicine in New York City* 2012. <http://www.everydayhealth.com/longevity/0530/optimism-laughter-may-bring-long-life.aspx > Web. 3 July 2014.

Chen, Daryl. (2014). The RD interview: Sonia Sotomayor. *Reader's Digest.* White Plains, New York: The Reader's Digest Association. 28-30. Print.

Honey, Michael K. (1963). *The King's Legacy: All Labor Has Dignity.* Boston: Beacon Press.
Print.

Idio, I. (2005). "Before My Journey Ends." *Expressions: American Poetry Society.* American Poets. 61. Print.

Laughter and anti-aging. (2013*). Best Skin Tighteners.* < http://www.humor-laughter.com/anti-agingandlaughter.html> Web. 3 July 2014.

Lehrman, Lewis. (2013). *Lincoln "by Littles."* Lehrman Institute, USA. Print.

Mrs. Unah. (1958). "The Story of the Greedy Hunter." Oral Story Time at Ibiaku Uruan Primary School: Akwa Ibom State, Nigeria.

Obama, Barrack. (2006.). *The Audacity of Hope.* New York: Three Rivers Press. Print.

Ostern, J. (2010). *Every Day A Friday.* New York: Hachette Book Group, 304-305. Print.

Perls, Thomas. (1994-2012). "The New England centenarian study." Corrected Ed. Boston University. < http://en.wikipedia.org/wiki/New_England_Centenarian_Study> Web. 3 July 2014.

Pope Francis. (2015). "Speaking of Education." *Virginia Education Journal.* 5. Print.

SearchYahoo.com. *Map Akwa Ibom State with Local Government* Areas, including Mbiaya Uruan. http://www.

akwaibomnewsonline.com/popups/akwa-ibom statemap.php. http://www.akwaibomnewsonline.Com/popups/akwa-ibom-state-map.php. web. 9 July 2015.

Wikipedia, the free encyclopedia. http://en.wikipedia.org. Web. 11 July 2014.

Wikipedia, the free encyclopedia. *Sixth and Seventh Books of Moses.* <http://en.wikipedia.org/wiki/Sixth_and_Seventh _Books_of_Moses> Web. 3 Aug. 2014.

APPENDIX A:
AN OVERVIEW OF
MBIAYA URUAN, AKWA
IBOM STATE, NIGERIA

Location:

- Uruan Local Government Area occupies a large landmass. It situates between latitude 6° 40` and longitude~ 7° 20` E in the North and West. It is bounded in the East by Odukpani

  Local, Government Area in Cross River State; in the South by Okobo Local Government Area; in the West by Nsit Atai and Ibesikpo Asutan Local Government Areas; and in the North by Itu Local Government Area.

- Mbiaya village is located in the Northern section of Uruan clan.

Current Population

Males	Females		TOTAL:
62,897	55,403		118,300

Natural Resources:
- Mineral deposits, e.g. crude oil, Silicon/glass sand, natural gas, sulfur nitrate, limestone and clay deposits

- **Commerce**
  Fishing, farming, trading, clay molding, arts and crafts, canoe/boat building

Paramount Ruler (lifetime ruler ship)
- His Royal Highness/HRM Edidem Effiong Bassey Asuquo Ekanem

Language/Dialect
- **Ibibio & Efik**

* Source: 2006 National Census of Nigeria

APPENDIX B:
MY BOOKS AND POETRY:

1. *Effective School Leadership: A Handbook for Aspiring and Experienced Leaders*, published in 2004.
2. *How to Eliminate Achievement Gap without Leaving Any Child Behind,* published in 2007
3. Poem: BEFORE MY JOURNEY ENDS @2005
4. *IGNATIUS EKPENYONG IDIO, SR.*

A Memoir: The Intriguing Journey of My Life (to be published in 2016 or posthumously)

These books are available at: www.authorhouse.com or 1-800-280-7715 or 1-800-839-8640 and at major book stores such as Barnes & Nobles and at Amzon.com.

APPENDIX C:
LANDED PROPERTY IN AKWA IBOM STATE, NIGERIA

I owned three landed property:

1. A townhouse located at 5475 Middlebourne Lane, Centreville, Virginia 20120 – The home was originally bought by my late wife Edemekong E. Idio which I inherited after her death.
2. A 3-bedroom flat at No. 6 Urua Udofia Street, Ewet Road, Uyo – the house is occupied by my senior brother, Dr. Calixtus Idio and his first wife Josephine Idio (Mma Nsa) and their children
3. A piece of land at Ewet Itam – which I intended to build a house on the land, but I did not have the money to continue the construction beyond the foundations begun on the plot. Also, after I became an American citizen in 2001, I decided against continuing with the building construction. The land is used by Dr. Calixtus and his wives for farming
4. A piece of land at Industrial Estate along Itu road. The land is used by Dr. Calixtus and his wives for farming.

APPENDIX D:
PHOTOS AND ARTIFACTS

This is a photo of me and Edemekong taken right after our traditional marriage reception in 2000 at Nsit Ubium Village, Akwa Ibom State of Nigeria.

Family Photo L-R:
Ignatius, Sr.; Francisca, Edemekong, Ignatius, Jr.

This is our photos in Nigerian traditional attires.

Family Photo Back L-R:
Edemekong, Francisca, Ignatius, Sr. & Front: Ignatius, Jr.

Dr. Ignatius Idio, Sr. is blessed by his elder brother, Dr. Calixtus Idio after the wedding.

Ignatius, Sr. and Elder Brother, Calixtus

These are my father and mother-in-laws when they were living with us in the US.

Father and Mother-in-laws: Chief Joseph & Madam Ekanem Esema

This photo shows Ignatius, Jr. (Iggy) with his baritone instrument at Centreville High School Marching Band in 2014.

Marching Band: Ignatius, Jr. Baritone Player

Francisca (Frankie: Center) performing at the Akwa Ibom State Rain Bow Cultural Dance Group in Washington, D.C. U.S.A.

Cultural Dance Performance: Francisca in the middle

Dr. Ignatius Idio, Sr. Posed after earning his degree in Educational Leadership from the University of Sarasota in Florida, USA in 2000. Well Done!

Graduation: Doctorate Degree in Educational Leadership, 2000

Photo of Ignatius Idio, Jr. at his High School Graduation in 2014 at the GMU Patriot Center.

Graduation: Ignatius, Jr. CVHS 2014

Ignatius, Jr. & Francisca

Ignatius, Jr. & Francisca

Ignatius, Sr. & Edemekong

Ignatius, Jr. & Francisca

Picture of My Father (Dad): Chief Francis Ekpenyong Idio
He belongs to the Ages.

Teacher EVER.... Thank
YOU ROCK!!! YOU~
FROM
THE SMITH
Happy Teacher FAMILY
~

Apprecation
Day!

HAVE A GREAT DAY!

We feel fortunate that you were Rachel's teacher this year ☺ Thank you for your support + encouragement. Have a great summer — I'll miss your fieldtrips!! Olivia + Greg

Dear Dr. Idio,
Thank you for being
my teacher this year
I enjoyed being in your
class,

Love,
Rachel

ADDENDUM

Times were when Nigeria enjoyed good living conditions in the first republic after its independence from Great Britain in 1960. Nigeria established good schools in most cities, workable healthcare system in several of the cities and local government areas in the country. Nowadays, we have high unemployment, high inflation, high crime rate, and an endemic corruption. In those days, there were distinct classes of citizens in Nigeria, namely, the upper class, the middle class, and the lower class. Lately, Nigerian currency is currently at a low value and the rate of exchange to the US currency is at N750 Naira to $1.00 US dollar. In other words, Nigerian currency is not acceptable by many Nigerians and some foreigners when they trade or do business with Nigeria. Many people prefer the dollar to Naira. Any Nigerian born in the 1950s-1960s would have experienced the same thing that I did. Majority of the citizens live in abject poverty. It is fair to say that, Nigeria is an oil producing nation and a member of the OPEC countries. Nigeria has other natural resources such as copper, manganese, iron, palm fruits. The discovery of crude oil swayed the federal government not to diversify the resources. Instead, it focused on the crude oil production and export to earn revenue. Today, about 90% of the revenue comes from the oil export. With lack of employments, many Nigerians resort to crimes to earn a living. Some of my relatives including my elder brother duped me and embezzled the fund that I transferred to them to use to renovate my old dilapidated house in 2023.

THE ORIGINAL FAMILY OF THE IDIOS

I describe the *Original* Family of the Idios in the following terms.

1. It consisted of our father, late Chief Francis Ekpenyong Udokang Akpandem Akana Uyoko, a polygamist (see Memoir, Chapter 1, p.1 of this text, 2015)
2. It comprised of our mother, late Akon Udoenang Okpok kpenyong Idio (see Memoir, Chapter 1, p.2)
3. It comprised of 19 children including this author from his four wives (see Memoir, Chapter 1, p.1 of this text, 2015)
4. Several grandchildren

My elder brother and two of his children (my Niece and my Nephew duped me and swindled some of the dollars I transferred from the US to use to restore the dilapidated house. I believe these relatives became fraudsters and swindlers due to the lack of employment. Some of them had professional degrees in the legal field. They victimized me because I worked and lived in the US for several years. They used me as a source of income to support them. I forgave but I will not forget what they did to me. My elder brother made plans to sell my property behind my back. An in-law informed me before my brother could sell the property. I made a **WILL** for my American-born children to inherit the property. I submitted the WILL to a Probate Court in Uyo Akwa Ibom State. I feel that to forgive and forget is divine but to forgive and forget not is human.

EXTENDED FAMILY OF THE IDIOS

My nucleus family consists of the parents, Dr. Ignatius Okon Epkenyong Idio, Ms. Mary Solomon Idio, the mother of Victoria and Stephanie and the Late Mrs. Edemekong Esema Idio, the mother of Ignatius, Junior and Francisca.

My Children: Victoria Inyang Idio, Stephanie Akon Idio, Ignatius Ini-Obong Idio Jr., and Francisca Mfonobong Idio (all are American citizens as well as Nigerian citizens.) They are successful adults in their unique ways.

From a humble circumstance, I transitioned to America in 1999 to further my studies beyond high school education. I earned my Bachelor's, Master's, and Ph.D/Ed.D degrees in America. America provided the opportunities for me to achieve my academic and career goals. America is a land of opportunities. If people set goals and work hard, they will achieve their goals. That is to say, they will achieve the "American Dream."

QUESTION

Where are heaven and Earth located? Many people think that Heaven and Earth are in the sky. Heaven and hell are here on Earth. These are the proofs. When we do or experience positive things in our daily lives such as love, peace, marriage, and treat other people as we treat ourselves, we are in heaven. In contrast, when we kill our fellow humans, or invade other nations and bomb them to cause humanitarian disasters like President Putin did in Ukraine (Feb 7, 2023), we are in hell.

KNOWLEDGE PHILOSOPHY WISDOM AND INTUITION OF THE AUTHOR (8 OCT. 2013)

People desire these three basic elements for survival, food, taste and sex. Philosophically, this author believes that there is death in life, and there is life in death.

A WORD ABOUT ARTIFICIAL INTELLIGENCE OR AI

A few philosophers started the artificial intelligence (AI) in antiquity, with myths, allegories, and rumors of the AI. They "attempted to describe the process of human thinking as the mechanical manipulation of symbols in the invention of the programmable digital computer in the 1940s, a machine based on the abstract essence of mathematical reasoning. This device and the ideas behind it inspired a handful of scientists to begin seriously discussing the possibility of building an electronic brain" (Wikipedia, the free encyclopedia (see Computer disambiguation https://en.wikipedia.org/wiki/Computer (disambiguation)

In "1850, Charles Babbage, an English mechanical engineer, and polymath, originated the concept of a programmable computer. He was known as the "father of the computer" [22]. He conceptualized and invented the first mechanical computer in the early 19th century."

In the 21st century America, "a few researchers founded AI at a workshop held on the campus of Dartmouth College in the summer of 1956. [1] Those who attended the training would become the leaders of AI research for decades. Many of them predicted that a machine as intelligent as human would exist in no more than a generation, and they received millions of dollars to make this vision come true. [2]" https://en.wikipedia.org/wiki/Timeline_of_artificial_intelligence

For a fact, AI will enhance and disrupt the facet of human life in many ways. For better or for worse AI is here to stay.

PREDICTIONS ABOUT TERM LIMITS FOR THE US CONSTITUTION AMENDMENT XXII

"In the United States, term limits (aka) rotation in office restrict the number of terms an officeholder may serve at the federal and state level ..." https?//ballotpedia.orgTerm_limits_in_the_United_States"constitutioncenter.org › amendments › amendment-xxii22[nd] Amendment - Two-Term Limit on Presidency | Constitution ...

Simply put, "The Twenty-Second **(Amendment XXII)** states that

Section 1

"No person shall be elected to the office of the President more than twice, and no person who has held the office of President, or acted as President, for more than two years of a term to which some other person was elected President shall be elected to the office of the President more than once."

Section 2

This article shall be inoperative unless it shall have been ratified as an amendment to the Constitution by the legislatures of three-fourths of the several states within seven years from the date of its submission to the States by the Congress.

Thus, "The Twenty-second Amendment (Amendment XXII) to the United States Constitution limits the number of times a person can be elected to the office of President of the United States to two terms, and sets additional eligibility conditions for presidents who succeed to the unexpired terms of their predecessors. Congress approved the Twenty-second Amendment on March 21, 1947, and submitted it to the states ... Wikipedia" (February 27, 1951)

MY POLITICAL AFFILIATION AND THE WORLD INSPIRING PEOPLE IN 2016 & BEYOND

I describe myself as a Liberal-Conservative Voter in (2023 and beyond). These men and women from different continents demonstrated exemplary leadership qualities in their policies and stance in their countries and in the world at large.

On July 28, 2023. 03:12 PM (GMT) General Omar Tchiani, commander of Niger's presidential guards, appointed himself head of the new military government. He opposed the superpower European countries from exploiting the natural resources of African nations through neo-colonization or imperialism.

In 2021, the military leader of Chad, General Mahamat Idriss Déby became the interim president of Chad after his father died fighting alongside the opposition group or FACT rebels after the death of President Idriss Déby on April 19, l 2021. He restored law and order in the country.

In 2021, the military leader of Guinee, Mamady Doumbouya took over power in a coup, and was sworn in as president when he announced, "that the army had little choice but to seize power because of the rampant corruption, disregard for human rights, and economic mismanagement under the 83-year-old President Condé." The new president spoke at the Mohammed V Palace in Conakry to explain his mission to "refound the state" to write a new constitution, to tackle corruption, to change the electoral system, and to include "free, credible and transparent" elections, according to the AFP news agency". He promised to "respect all the national and international commitments to which the country has https://www.bbc.com/news/world-africa-58461971

On 9/4/2023, Gabon's military junta, General Brice Nguema was sworn in as the interim military leader in a coup. He Ousted President Ali Bongo Ondimba and accused him of election fraud and corruption since he began ruling the oil-rich but poverty-stricken nation nearly 14 years ago. As a result, several residents in the capital cities and embraced the soldiers on the street. He pledged to stop foreign European governments from exploiting the natural resources, including copper, crude oil, and other resources in Gabon. (https://www.cnn.com/2023/08/31/africa/gabon-military-coup-explainer-intl-hnk/index.html)

https://www.abc.net.au/news/2023-09-05/gabon-coup-leader-nguema-sworn-in-as-interim-president/102814124?utm_campaign=newsweb-article-new-share-null

Angela Merkel, the First female Chancellor of Germany for 16 years and a strong leader and was named Forbes' World Most Powerful woman for 10 consecutive years https://www.thegrowthfaculty.com

Michelle Bachelet, First woman President of Chile. She worked to protect the rights of all people around the world https://www.aramco.com

Malala Yousafzai, a Nobel Prize Laureate. She overcame an assassination attempt by the Taliban in Pakistan. She supported the right of girls and women to attend schools.

In 2021, the military leader of Burkina Faso, Ibrahim Traoré - took over power in a coup. He stood against France and Belgium to stop them from exploiting Uranium and other natural resources from Niger. (Read the link below for additional https://en.wikipedia.org/wiki/Ibrahim_Traoré

In April 2021, the military leader of Sudan, General Abdel Fattah al-Burhan took over leadership in a coup. He supported the pro-democracy groups and encouraged them to demonstrate in the streets. He planned to return the leadership to a civilian government (Follow the link for more information) https://www.cnn.com/2021/10/25/africa/sudan-coup-explained-intl-cmd/index.html

ANNOTATED BIBLIOGRAPHY OF YOUNG LEADERS ACROSS THE GLOBE

Since 2020-2023, the African youths have demonstrated support for the military seizure of power in Niger, Mali, Garbon, etc. The youths are looking for liberators and leaders who will protect the natural resources in Africa and prevent the pillage of the resources by the super power nations such as the UK, the USA, China, Germany, France, and many others. (https://www.msn.com/en-us/news/world/why-african-youths-are-in-support-of-military-coup-obasanjo/ar-AA1gWnZL

1. Mr. Julius Melana of South Africa - advocated for the African Socialist economic system with African characteristics. He predicted the downfall of the European capitalist system in Africa.
2. Professor Patrick Lumumba of Kenya - made several speeches in favor of the transformation of Africa into one African state from tribal groups to African nations and the protection of the resources for the Africans.
3. President Lazarus of Malawi - spoke about and encouraged the current African leaders to preserve the integrity of resources to pass on a better continent to current and future generations.

In 2023, President Muhamed Tinibu - took office as the new president of Nigeria. He promised to bring changes that will help all Nigerians to overcome decades of hardships, crimes and corruption in the country. All Nigerians should support his projects.

In 2021, President Joe Biden and Vice President Kamala Harris (1st African American woman) were elected President and Vice President of the US. They created jobs, tackled the pandemics caused by the coronavirus, reduced inflation. He promised to control COVID-19 viruses, and supported the invention of vaccines through the Centers for Disease Control or CDC. They also provided vaccines to developing countries to help fight the pandemics.

Former First Lady Rosalynn Carter died on 11/19/2023 (CNN) at the age of 96 in Plains, Georgia. She was an activist who "destigmatize" mental health (Pres. Bush) and founder of the Carter Center in Atlanta and the Habitat for Humanity foundation. She was a model for Marriage relationship. She was married to Former President Carter for 75 years.

In 2023, German Chancellor Olaf Scholz pledged to protect Germany's Jews in the rise of anti-Semitism. She delivered speeches at a Berlin synagogue to commemorate the anniversary. This particular synagogue had been targeted with Molotov cocktails just last month. Chancellor Scholz has committed to safeguarding Germany's Jewish community, especially in the face of increasing anti-Semitism following the Israel-Hamas war. (https://www.msn.com/en-us/news/world/israel-hamas-war-german-place-by-israels-side-scholz/ar-AA1ikIcU)

In 2023, Chinese President Xi Jinping visited Australia during a "very successful" meeting in Beijing. The president of China works with other leaders in support of peace in the world. China invested in infrastructural development projects in several developing countries around the world.

Prime Minister Anthony Albanese has invited Chinese President Xi Jinping to visit Australia after he visited Beijing. The Australian government is against Putin's invasion of Ukraine in 2023.

King Abdullah II of Jordan met with Russian President Vladimir Putin when he visited Jordan to discuss prospects for the Israeli–Palestinian peace process, Iran's nuclear program, and violence in Iraq. Abdullah the II supports peace and a two-state solution for Israel and Lebanon (wikipedia.com)

In 2022, Michel AOUN was elected the President of Lebanon. He supports the two-state solution to create an independent country for the people of Lebanon and the crisis between Israel and Lebanon.

In 2023, the President of Egypt, Abdel Fattah al-Sisi - allowed the people of Gaza and other foreign citizens to move south from Northern Gaza when the Prime Minister of Israel ordered them to flee to the south of Gaza. The President of Egypt allowed the fleeing Lebanese to pass through into Egypt. He allowed the flow of humanitarian relief materials to pass into Egypt after Israel bombed a hospital in Gaza.

ABOUT THE AUTHOR

Dr. Ignatius E. Idio, Sr. is the author of *How to Eliminate Achievement Gap Without Leaving Any Child Behind: A Handbook of Strategies and Best Practices,* which was published in 2007. He also wrote and published the *Effective School Leadership: A Handbook for Aspiring and Experienced Leaders* in 2004. Dr. Idio taught public schools in Shreveport, Louisiana, Fairfax County, and Prince William County, Virginia. He also served as an adjunct faculty member at Northern Virginia Community College or NOVA, in Manassas, Virginia for several years. In 2013, Dr. Idio was awarded a certificate in Appreciation and Recognition for Continuous and Loyal Service for Ten Years at NOVA. Dr. Idio lives in Centreville, Virginia with his son, Ignatius I. Idio Jr. and daughter, Francisca M. Idio, together with the mother of his children, Edemekong Esema Idio (a registered nurse), from 1994 until she died of breast cancer on 6 May 2012.

INSPIRATION

*The world will continue to evolve and progress
if knowledge is not static or squirrel away.
(Idio, 2015).*

INDEX

Federal Ministry of Labor (FML), 34

Five broomsticks, 8

General Murtala Ramat Mohammed, 63

George W. Bush, 64

Global community, 64

Global interconnectivity, 65

Good Samaritan, 29, 37

Great philosopher, 7

Groundnut or Apios tuberosa, 16

Hemorrhage, 6

Ibiaku Uruan, 1

Ibibio (Efik), 15

Idio Shrine, 5-6

Impermanent, 82, 85

Inalienable rights, 62

Indira Gandhi, 64

Ingersoll Elementary School, 30, 31

Investment, 12, 13

Judson Fundamental Magnet School, 30

Kellwood Mattress Company, 29

Magical incantations, 3

Mancala, 25

Manifestations, 8

Mbiaya Uruan, vii, ix, 3-4, 94, 97

Medicine man, 12

Mohandas Karamchand Gandhi, 63

National Census Board (NCB), 34

Nelson Rolihlahla Mandela, 64

Nigeria-Biafra Civil War, 12

Nonviolent civil disobedience, 63

Nsa Isong, 25-26

Omnipotent Decider, 52

Omniscient, 60

Outside interference, 52

Peace and tranquility, 66

Pneumonia, 40

Political philosophy and beliefs, 65

Primary Six School Leaving Examinations, 23

Private meeting, 50

Pronunciamento, 62

Psychological destruction, 67

Ignatius Idio is grateful to have lived his entire adult life after high school in the United States. Dr. Idio is also grateful he had the opportunity to earn his BA, MS, and EdD/PhD degrees in the states. He is equally grateful to give back to his community by teaching students in public schools and college. He still loves his birth country, Nigeria.

Printed in the United States
by Baker & Taylor Publisher Services